RICH BEFORE 40

PAZ ITZHAKI-WEINBERGER

Rich Before 40
Paz Itzhaki-Weinberger

Copyright © 2018 Paz Itzhaki-Weinberger

Translation from the Hebrew: Itzhak Solstzi
Contact: paz@itzhaki-weinberger.com

ISBN: 978-965-7724-42-2

RICH
BEFORE 40

THE ULTIMATE GUIDE TO WEALTH

PAZ ITZHAKI-WEINBERGER

Contents

About the Author

Attorney Paz Itzhaki-Weinberger, born in Israel (1980), serves today as chairman and CEO of the Israeli company he founded – IWC (Itzhaki-Weinberger Consultants Ltd.) – in the fields of technological consulting, data protection and investments in patents and intellectual property. Paz also heads the PIWLAW law firm, which he founded in Tel Aviv. He is a member of the bar association in Israel, the US, England and Wales. He is also a member of the advisory committees of some of the best startup companies in the Israeli economy.

Formerly he was a security expert and a senior software development engineer for Microsoft Corporation, at the company's Israeli development center – Microsoft Israel Research and Development (ILDC). Before that he was a security expert, developer, researcher and security content manager at Gteko – an international high-tech company with offices in the US, Japan, and in Israel. Gteko was acquired by Microsoft Corporation in 2006 – as was publicized in the global media – for some USD 121 million.

Paz is among the pioneers in the field of data communications in Israel, even before the Internet era: already in the 1990s, while still a teenager, he started HobbitNet – one of the largest data communications networks (BBS) in Israel which operated across the country. While doing this he was also running diversified IT businesses.

During his military service, he held a series of technological functions in the elite technology unit of the Intelligence Corps – Unit 8200. His last function in the Unit was that of chief technology officer in one of the operations centers of the unit. He was discharged from service in the standing army (as an outstanding officer) in early 2004 and is still serving in the reserves.

He acquired his academic education at two Israeli universities: Tel Aviv University and the Open University, in various courses – among them computer sciences, the Japanese language, and law. He is continuing advanced studies concurrent with his various occupations.

First and foremost, he is a prominent lawyer and businessman, but also a skilled technology expert, proficient in numerous subjects in the field of computers while specializing in four areas: data communications, managing software projects, patents, and data and cyber security .

In addition, Paz has been undertaking numerous activities – as a volunteer and otherwise – and was even sent to Singapore and to the Philippines to represent Israel on behalf of the Israeli Ministry of Foreign Affairs. Between his various occupations he finds the time to write books on different subjects. This is his first published work. "The Ultimate Guide to Wealth – Live Well and Become Rich Before 40" is about Paz's life philosophy and has a strong business orientation. It was written to provide useful tools for achieving abundance.

It might be worth mentioning something about the author's early beginnings. Paz lost his mother when he was only ten, and was later abandoned by his father, who ultimately cut off all ties with Paz and with Paz's brother and sister, following his remarriage.

The nationwide computer businesses started by Paz as a boy were a far cry from the stories of the boy who amuses himself by trying to become rich. Quite the opposite: they were started to provide a livelihood and sustenance. Paz, who was and still is considered one of the most outstanding officers in Unit 8200 of the Intelligence Corps, was recognized as a "lone soldier" due to the above circumstances, during his military service. He was an orphan, *de facto*, from a young age. His beginnings were therefore far from pleasant and he started from a very difficult economic situation, without the normal support of a family. Nevertheless, thanks to his persistence in developing and closely following the principles presented in this book, his life trajectory has hit upon the right path – the road upwards – "Out of the depths and on to the top."

Foreword

I first thought about writing this book at the cemetery, of all places.

It happened on the anniversary of the death of my dear mother Hanna, of blessed memory, who passed away suddenly and tragically at a young age. As usual, quite a few people were present, even though many years had passed. My mother was a wonderful woman. She left a deep impression and touched the lives of many.

At the cemetery I was thinking to myself – will I have so many people come to my own memorial, many years after I pass? The answer to that question was very clear to me at the time: **No. Definitely no. Not a chance.** I'm a much less friendly person, compared to my mother. At the time, I thought that it would be a great accomplishment if several years after my demise a 'minyan' would still come to visit my grave…

But I was much more bothered by the understanding that even my dear mother, despite the intense impression she used to make on people and her influence upon them throughout her life, will be forgotten forever as time goes by, and certainly in a few generations' time – three or four, not more – there will be nobody to remember her. The only (and perhaps most important) legacy that she left are us, her children. It may seem quite natural, but in some way, I was very bothered by that thought at the time. I was thinking – "I don't even have that yet. I have no children, I have yet to start my own family" (I married and became a father several years later); "the only heritage that I will leave (so I thought) will be a mountain of cash (not big enough in my view… let's call it 'a small hill of cash' for the sake of the matter), that will certainly be consumed quickly by my happy successors…" It was then that I first thought of leaving something else after me, something that will be remembered for generations to come.

The decision to actually buckle down and write the book was finally made in London (by the way – I also finalized the book in London, during a fundraising campaign for a new startup, in June 2008, and I took several more years before deciding that I actually wanted to publish it and present it to the reader). I was on a business trip and used a free moment to go to the Tate Museum, where I saw an exhibition of the works of Frida Kahlo.

And then it hit me. Just like Mexican painter Frida Kahlo, there are so many people, perhaps thousands of people, who have left an everlasting legacy behind them, a heritage that millions of other people know about, who live according to or are influenced by, even dozens, hundreds or thousands of years after they die.

In the same context, of course many of my own concepts and ideas came from books, whose authors passed away ages ago, and not only from the personal experiences that I had during my lifetime. I see reading as one of the most powerful experiences available to human existence. It is a way to connect with the past, with other ideas and other concepts, and sometimes to really "hold a conversation" with those no longer with us.

The one thing these people have in common, whose heritage has remained engraved in the consciousness of an entire public, is that they not only spoke or acted, they also wrote and documented, or were documented by others. In this way, they disseminated their message to further and further generations.

Documenting, writing, leaving the message – these are key to an everlasting heritage.

It was then that I resolved to write this book, which in many ways may become my legacy; something of value that I will leave behind when I leave this world one day. The essence of this book is not money and greed – please do not misunderstand this. The core of the book is teaching and imparting a change and improvement to the lives of many, while enriching their spiritual and material worlds.

The purpose of this book is to bring you, the reader, a change for the better; to rescue you or your children, who are trapped in the cobwebs woven by society in the frantic day-to-day race for survival and existence, and to lead you to material wealth. Abundance will free you from the frantic ways of the world and liberate you from the shackles of the mortgage and the other day-to-day economic constraints.

I believe that spiritual wealth comes with the material one, and that will be my gift.

I hope that the guidelines in this book will percolate into your head, and maybe into your children's consciousness as well. I hope that they will help you become wealthy and reach economic well-being at a young age.

What will you decide to do at that point, when you manage to become rich? Will you really enrich your spiritual world, rather than simply indulge in the pleasures that money brings and only realize your non-spiritual desires?

That decision is totally yours.

One last matter before we start: If you forget me after you read this book and implement its principles, that's all right. I feel that I did what I had to do, not only because you bought my book with your hard-earned money and contributed (if only a little) to my own (or to my family's) economic well-being. I will be glad, knowing that at least your bank manager is joyful and smiles at you from ear to ear every time you meet, and that this is happening at least in part thanks to me; and that your baby is sleeping quietly in his crib without you having to fear that he will lose his home, food or shelter, or having to worry about financing his academic studies. I will even see in each sip of martini, that you will enjoy while seated by your private swimming pool in the new house that you will have acquired, a toast of sorts in my honor (and if the book is read and remains relevant long after my demise – a toast in my memory).

Finally, it is important for me to dedicate this book, with all of my heart, to my two beloved and amazing daughters, Abigail and Noa. Wise and precious daughters, lovely and benevolent, who have taught me the meaning of humility and have totally altered my objectives and priorities (only for the best!), and of course to my wife, who always supports me, in good times and bad - Dr. Mor Lurie-Weinberger, a virtuous and highly accomplished woman and one of the most impressive people in existence. I am privileged to have won such a marvelous spouse!

All right, that's enough chit-chat. Let's get down to business. At this point, many of you are certainly thinking: "I've had enough of this bore… show me the money!"

And so we begin…

Paz Itzhaki-Weinberger

Israel 2016

CHAPTER 1

Insurance and Securities – Critical Tools to Guarantee That You Become Rich

I will start the first chapter with a question that I see as central: **How does a person become rich?**

The simplest and commonest way is probably by being born to the correct family. If you come from the British royal family or are a Rothschild, you will probably receive vast amounts of property at some point in your life by reason of your birth, and even if you mess up and repeatedly make rather horrible economic decisions during your lifetime, you will find it very difficult to shake the strong financial foundation of your family.

If you are reading this book, you probably do not come from such a family (and if you do, you probably see it as just a collection of funny anecdotes, as you never underwent and will never undergo the various tribulations described in it). All that is left for you to do is to quietly sigh (ruefully perhaps) and find consolation in the fact that even though you did not come from a well-to-do noble family, at least you were blessed with a loving family that supports you and accepts you with all of your defects (but even this is quite uncertain in today's far-from-simple reality…).

Another way to become rich is to win a large amount of money, for example in the lottery. If I were you I wouldn't count on that method. You can buy a lottery ticket from time to time, just for fun, but don't develop expectations. Your chances of actually winning the grand prize are similar to your chances of having lunch on July 15th at a particular hour, having a sudden heart attack at that exact same time, then being struck twice by lightning in a thunderstorm that suddenly takes place in the middle of the summer, and then coming out alive…

My grandfather used to say that he wins the lottery every week, and has so again and again for years. I asked him how that was possible, to which he answered that he simply does not buy a ticket. Every week that he refrained from buying the ticket, he won the price of the ticket. Just for illustration, let us assume that a weekly lottery ticket costs $10. In a year, this is an investment of $520. After forty years the amount becomes about $20,000. With modest interest rates and offsetting small wins, this is actually on average an amount of about $35,000 that a person will pay to the lottery company during his life, if he regularly buys the tickets.

Another accepted way to become rich in the Western and capitalistic world is described as "hard work." My life experience shows that it's very hard (if not impossible) to become rich through work. The number of people who became rich by working is smaller than the number of the lottery winners. What does that say about your own chances?

Normally, the system in Western countries is devised in a way that allows one to reach economic prosperity through hard work, but only within the confines of the upper middle class. Through hard work, one can make a respectable living for oneself and for one's family – perhaps with a few luxuries.

Real wealth? The system is built in a way that renders this task almost impossible.

So far, we have examined three methods for becoming rich – being born rich, winning the lottery and working hard – and we saw that we cannot rely upon the latter two, and the first one was already decided for us in advance. This method has probably skipped 99.9% of the readers of this book.

There is, of course, a much more realistic method, with much higher chances of success – and that is marrying into wealth. A person who is attractive enough, who knows in which circles to circulate and how to market oneself, has definite chances of meeting a partner who would radically change his (or her) economic situation. This is also not a simple method, as wealthy people generally spend their time in very exclusive circles, and wealthy families have an unwritten rule, a glass ceiling of sorts: "money goes with money," i.e. – one only marries a partner whose economic status is similar. Nevertheless, books, gossip columns and Hollywood films are all full of such stories, and this certainly seems to be a more promising alternative to winning the lottery or to working hard, as the case may be.

This book does not discuss this option at all. I was never a good matchmaker. I'm also not a greedy person and I never tried this method (and at my advanced age and considering my current economic standing, I will probably never start). I chose to marry out of love and I'm 100% happy with this decision!

There is of course the possibility of generating personal equity through crime, but I will of course leave this method completely aside. This method carries ethical and moral problems, and involves numerous risks that diminish the chances for success. It is also a derivative of having chosen a very specific type of occupation.

Later in this book you will see that one can generate wealth (immense wealth) also in other ways than those described above, even from a bad starting point in life – and with much higher chances of success than with the other methods that we described here. Some will certainly say that the method that I will later present involves extreme sacrifices and obsessive behavior for years, and that it is therefore much harder than "hard work." Nevertheless, the chances of success for those who follow that path are, in my opinion, higher than with any other method, so long as the person traveling the path is determined to reach his goal and operates with it in mind in any interaction he has in life.

Now, enough talking about becoming rich in general. In this chapter we will delve into the most important tools to guarantee your success – **insurance and securities.**

WHAT IS INSURANCE AND WHY IS IT IMPORTANT?

Upon hearing this word, many of us immediately think about powerful and wealthy insurance companies, situated in huge buildings with glass and marble fixtures and employing executives who pocket untold salaries. These companies are portrayed as being capable of collecting their premiums from their clients very successfully, but when a disaster really occurs (or any insurance incident – these are generally unfortunate and unpleasant events for the policyholder, for which he desperately needs the help of the insurance company, and which are the reason he purchased insurance in the first place), they start to steamroll their clients with pressure and legal measures in order to diminish the amount that they will have to pay them, or to avoid paying altogether.

In actual fact, it is clear to many that purchasing insurance is at times tantamount to buying "an entry ticket to court," not to guaranteeing the payment itself – but this is sometimes enough. Sometimes even this statement is inaccurate, as I will shortly explain here.

For these reasons, many see insurance as an unnecessary commodity. This is especially true in Israel, where the idea "this won't happen to me" is prevalent. Most Israelis spend their lives thinking they will be spared any of those disasters that they hear about in the media, or first-hand from acquaintances and friends, throughout their lifetimes. Therefore, they will also obviously never pay insurance premiums and would only benefit from this, the exception being where the regulator imposed upon them a compulsory insurance (in Israel, a good example for this is car insurance against bodily damages, which is an absolutely obligatory insurance and is prescribed by law for any car owner).

Nevertheless, insurance can be a wonderful arrangement, at least theoretically. To illustrate the importance of insurance – let's take a village with 2,000 residents. Once a year, a fire strikes the village and one family loses its home and all of its property and remains destitute. Let us assume that the average family property, lost in the fire, is worth $200,000. If every resident of the village lends a hand and contributes $8.33 every month ($100 a year) to a fund that would compensate those whose house was burnt, every time a fire consumes someone's house, that person will receive full compensation for his damages. This is the purpose of insurance in a nutshell. Every resident knows that at a minimal cost of $8.33 a month, he actually frees himself of a risk that might destroy his life (a damage of $200,000 that he saved his entire life). This is actually a tool that provides a social safety net for the individual.

The actual cost of insurance is, of course, a bit higher and not necessarily optimal. One has to pay the salaries of those who arrange the entire operation (the insurance agents) and actually collect the money. One should also collect further amounts, to make sure that there is enough money in the cashbox for worse years, in which (for example) four people lose their house at once. There are also litigation costs and the costs of defending against all manner of insurance fraud scams (yes, there are also crooks and swindlers among us – we do not live in a Utopian society), and maybe most importantly in today's reality – one needs to generate profits for demanding shareholders…

and yet – let us say that instead of $100 a year, one is required to pay $200 a year ($16.66 a month) due to all of the variables presented above. This is still, probably, a reasonable price to pay for eliminating the risks, **and as we will see later in this chapter, if you want to make sure that you do become rich – you must purchase the suitable insurance policies.**

THE CONNECTION BETWEEN INSURANCE AND GUARANTEEING YOUR ENRICHMENT

Every person is born with a certain economic potential. Beyond the invaluable worth of one's life and enjoyment thereof, every individual works, produces, earns and of course also consumes services and products, thereby helping other people realize their own inherent economic potential and their own productivity, and helps set vast economic processes in motion.

Even if we take a person who earns salaries that are at the bottom of the pay table throughout his life – the minimum wage (let us assume that this is $1,000 a month, to make it easier to calculate) – and who never makes any progress or improves his income level, we will see that during an average 40-year working career he will manage to generate more than half a million dollars of income.

However, those who are aware of their surroundings know that life is not a safe operation. Life is more like a trouble-strewn minefield, full of suffering and pain. One can die any moment due to a terrorist act. Some of us will fall victim to serious crimes. Very many of us will succumb to illness, while others will be killed in road accidents or natural disasters.

When a 20-year-old guy dies of cancer, this is also an economic disaster, ranging from the loss of $500,000 in income – the minimum – to millions of dollars. But one does not have to die in order to lose their economic potential. **Being handicapped may be a much heavier economic disaster than death.** A person who becomes handicapped and loses his earning capacity at the age of twenty not only loses his future revenues but also incurs heavy expenses of medical and nursing care that he would not have needed at all, were he to remain healthy. Once a productive person, he now becomes an economic burden, a "pit" that sucks in great expenses.

I believe that every person should strive to be insured against various disasters that are reasonably likely to occur. The lack of such insurance may lead to one losing the potential of becoming rich.

Wherever I present this opinion, in which I believe with all of my heart, I run into criticism across the board, especially from people who completely reject the idea of life insurance. Many people tell me that all is good and well, a person who dies young and leaves life insurance behind him does become a millionaire and on the face of it realizes his economic potential (if only partially) – but he actually derives no enjoyment of the fact, because he is dead!

Life insurance may perhaps be an extreme example, but I still believe in it. The policyholder knows that no matter what, even if he dies, his inherent economic potential will be realized, at least partially. Life insurance becomes especially important when the deceased has surviving family members – and even more so when these are economically dependent upon him. It is obviously impossible to compensate family members for the loss of their loved one, and no amount of money can adequately compensate for this. So why does one need life insurance at all? The purpose is not to enrich the relatives at the expense of the deceased (even though this does happen at times, depending on the insurance amount), but to free them from economic worries and troubles.

From personal experience, I can say that the death of a family member can thoroughly disintegrate a family. At times, some family members may become total wrecks, with no earning capacity. The insurance is there to compensate for that fact as well, affording economic welfare to the beneficiaries despite the tragic event.

In the context of enrichment, one does not only consider life insurances or insurance against a severe illness. There is a whole other series of (relatively cheap) insurances that protect, for example, real estate, the contents of a house and a vehicle. Just like with everything else in life, one should also not exaggerate with insurance – we all hope that we will not have to use it – we wish to only pay the premiums and not "enjoy" the benefits. The way I see it, everyone must insure themselves and purchase reasonable insurance policies against reasonable risks – death, severe illnesses and needing nursing care - and also against critical risks to important property, such as real estate and vehicles.

In the context of enrichment, the purpose of insurance is to guarantee that a sudden event does not interrupt a glorious success, and that it at least leaves the potential for success at the same level it was on the eve of the sudden event.

It is obvious that a person with the potential of becoming a multimillionaire, who dies at a young age due to a sudden incident, will not become rich without insurance (and as above, some will say that he will never become rich – but the way I see it, the economic potential is realized also when the successors become rich), and this is certainly the case with a severe illness.

Nevertheless, sometimes the potential for success is left untapped for quite another silly reason. Let us take a 35-year-old-man, healthy and fully alert. He worked and now has an apartment and reasonable savings. Now he can take a break from work for 2-3 years and start investing in ventures of his own. Let us say that he has a high enrichment potential in the next five years, but his dream may very well vanish due to a fire that would consume his apartment.

This man worked for 15 years in order to reach a reasonable economic condition, that allows him to take business risks and perhaps make strides, and one sunny day he goes back 15 years because he was not insured. He may very well have lost even more than 15 years now: some people might go into depression in this situation, due to the unfortunate event, and many others will have a hard time creating their erstwhile capital anew, being already older (also the age, in which one may expect success, will be deferred to a later date, way on the horizon).

THE TOOLBOX FOR CHAPTER ONE – INSURANCE AND SECURITIES

If you are relatively young, still not rich but planning to be, do yourselves a favor and listen to this piece of advice: dedicate a 5% chunk of your available (net) income to various insurance policies. This is a negligible price for your and your family's peace of mind, and for safeguarding your potential for success. Do not insure luxuries – insure only the essentials: health – insurance against severe illnesses, loss of working capacity, requiring nursing care and life insurance – and the most important assets – your residential apartment and its contents, and maybe also your car.

Remember: it is important to insure yourselves only against those incidents, where it is clear that if they occur, you will be unable to recover from them, or will require many years and considerable efforts to return to your original situation before the event.

Nevertheless, it is important to remember that insurance does not guarantee the actual realization of your potential and your enrichment. This already depends on you – but generally the insurance will allow you to keep that potential even when disaster strikes.

Sometimes, for example when one suffers severe disabilities, the actual potential may disappear or diminish, but the insurance will guarantee its monetary (if partial) realization, even without it being actually realized. If we take a person who had the potential of owning $10 million in capital at the end of his life, it may certainly be the case, that due to becoming handicapped at a young age he will actually realize only $2 million worth of revenues through insurance, but without the insurance he would not have realized his potential at all.

CHAPTER 2

Haters and Jealous People

We all know people, for whom it is important to have everyone they know, love them. Quite a few of us are even obsessively working on that, and for some of us this is such an important matter, that we experience distress when others are hostile or cold towards us, especially when we feel that our own behavior towards others is worthy and good.

If we think for a moment and try to find a common denominator for all of the people of this type whom we know (while leaving out spoiled successors or happy lottery winners), we may easily find one common denominator: **Not one of these people is rich.**

The rich among us know that not only is it impossible to have everybody love us, it is also undesirable. Moreover, the best warning sign that something is wrong, is a lack of haters. Even if at some stage of their lives it was important for rich people to have the environment love them, at some point along the way they forgot about this, which is one of the key factors in their success.

Every choice in life comes with a price, and the general equation says that **in order to have everybody love you, you will have to sacrifice your wealth and success.**

It is important for me to clarify this point: I am not saying that a successful, wealthy man cannot enjoy love. Quite the opposite. But he cannot enjoy love and a positive attitude from everyone around him. He also cannot go through life without haters, jealous people and other ill-wishers.

This rule does not only hold true for financial success, but for success in general. Many of us see this very human behavior as "the evil eye." If you have a wonderful, extraordinary romantic relationship, you will probably earn a generous portion of envy and jealousy. It is highly likely that someone will even methodically try to harm your relationship – whether to achieve a personal objective or to simply enjoy your defeat.

However, it is interesting to note that if you have a problematic relationship and your wife is not an attractive woman, it is rather the positive side of people that will manifest. When you hit rock bottom, it is poor form to hate you and of course there is no reason to envy you. In such situations, emotions such as mercy or a feeling of superiority come to the fore. If everybody around you wants to provide help and assistance – your condition is probably much worse than theirs. Very few people are truly noble, rise above personal interests and truly do not envy others.

It is important to understand that many of the haters and the jealous people are not evil. Usually their hatred, jealousy and negative emotions towards you are not occasioned by a feeling of revolt that you inspire in them, but from their own self-detest or disappointment of their more modest achievements, compared to yours. It is only natural for a person, who sees himself as successful and worthy, but who has unfortunately failed to reach significant achievements, to rejoice as his neighbor collapses, who did make it in life and who reached those same achievements that he desires – especially where he perceives his neighbor as less worthy of his high status than he is.

So far, we understand that if you have no haters and nobody is jealous of you – something must be wrong. There is no real reason to envy you because your condition is poor and there is no reason to hate you, because you are not doing anything of note in your life. Every great person in human history had many haters and objectors, and such resistance is a good sign. An exceptionally successful and extraordinary person, such as Shimon Peres of blessed memory, often creates a long line of haters and critics, both within and without, for countless years. It is doubtless that had he not been a highly active and accomplished person, none of these would trouble him.

On the other hand, and a very important point – there is no reason to create haters. It is absolutely undesirable to initiate such a move. It will come naturally with success, and in the right measure. It is much better to try and inspire the opposite feelings – the mercy and compassion of those around you. Try to emphasize your defects. Even a very successful person has defects. There are no perfect people and there is no perfect life. It is better to remain modest and emphasize how human you are on every occasion.

A rich and successful person, whose son is addicted to drugs, should not obscure the matter or bury it under the carpet. Quite the opposite. Beyond having to do everything possible, as a parent, to save his child from this problem, he should be openhearted about this. Potential haters may soften and say, for example, that even though they are not as wealthy as he is, their children are more successful. His problems will open a window for dialogue with his environment.

Will underscoring your negative qualities and defects turn every hater into a lover? Of course not. To further develop the example given above, those whose hatred emanates from envying the success of another, will be able to add fuel to the fire and say that this is a horrible parent, a man who has sacrificed his family on the altar of success and greed. As we already said, the existence of haters is a ne plus ultra indicator of success.

Another point worth remembering: some situations may easily create haters for you, and as we said, it is better to avoid creating enemies unnecessarily. Sometimes a person is at another's mercy, especially when dealing with officials in various authorities, or even when recruiting employees or during routine operations with government officials. Each of us, under certain circumstances, may find himself at another's mercy, at least in a certain context.

In such situations, one may generally assume that the official sitting in front of you has no personal interest to harm you, and therefore the matter may be managed in two main ways: one – a businesslike approach, sending you along your way as soon as possible; the other way – intentionally tripping you up (even when there is no need to do this). The person who acts like that while exercising his authority or taking some bureaucratic measure, often gets a sense of personal achievement and victory over his counterpart – that is to say, you.

Let us assume that a wealthy, successful and handsome individual, whose marriage is successful and whose children are even more successful, finds himself willy-nilly in a situation, in which he depends on another person on some issue – and this happens pretty often. The other person (being human) will be intrigued to find that under the veneer of success there lies a dark secret, and that he is the one who has managed to bring this secret to light – and maybe even to "shatter" this idyllic existence – if even for a short time, through imparting a particular even significant form of damage.

The more he emphasizes his success and conformity to the norms and shows himself to be positive and of high quality, the more the successful person may awaken the "rage" (or more precisely, the flaming jealousy) of the person charged with handling his affair, driving that person to make him fail, to put obstacles in his path and to encumber him with difficulties. In such a situation one would do well to conceal his achievements, show a lack of understanding and innocence and expose less flattering aspects of his character, in order to have his counterpart feel empathy (despite the great gap that may exist between them) and end the unpleasant situation as soon as possible. In some situations, even the strongest person does better by showing himself as being weak, the wealthiest (in assets) as poor (in other matters), and the wise, as a fool.

The truly wise person knows when he should present himself this way or that. I see the ability to show oneself as weak, maybe even to be actually weak in certain situations, without losing any of one's honor, as the clear sign of a strong person. It is safe to assume that such a person is much likelier to become rich.

THE TOOLBOX FOR CHAPTER TWO – HATERS AND JEALOUS PEOPLE

The very existence of haters and jealous people is an excellent indicator of success. Usually, an abundance of haters indicates an abundance of assets and/or significant success. Nevertheless, it is important not to create unnecessary haters. This does not mean that you have to invest great resources just to avoid creating haters, or in futile attempts to please everybody around you, but if you consistently avoid situations that would create haters for you, and they still emerge, it seems that you're on the right track.

It is true, in some situations (as we will see later), it is important to radiate success in order to truly succeed, but in many more situations it is precisely proper to show your defects, weaknesses and imperfections. By showing defects, you will not be perceived as defective. The result will often be the opposite: the defects will make you look more human, while hiding them will create antagonism and make you a target for hatred.

When you are a symbol of success and subject to hatred or jealousy, those around you strive to expose your defects and shame you, but when the defects are already exposed, people will generally show sympathy, perhaps mercy – which will lead to empathy. This will obviously not work when dealing with sworn (and vital) haters, such as those I have mentioned before.

CHAPTER 3

Accepting Death as Part of Life

According to a common adage, only two things are sure in life – death and income tax.

Well, many would disagree with the second part of this maxim (and I think that actually in recent years, as this area is enforced more and more tightly, fewer people challenge this statement, and rightly so!), but nobody can doubt the first part – if one thing is certain in life, it is the fact that it will end sooner or later.

Many of us abhor death, fear it, are reluctant to think about it. Most of us have a hard time imagining the day we will die, and we try to repress such thoughts as far as possible. Death brings us chills, and the effort to delay the end is among the fundamental principles of almost every living creature on Earth.

I see death as simply another part of life. This understanding – and the acceptance thereof – is a critical key for success and enrichment. Let me explain what I mean. Many of us hesitate to take risks of various types, simply due to fear of failure. The classical example: I have a wonderful idea that can lead me to success in business, in my view. To promote that idea, however, to register it as a patent and do everything involved in its implementation, I will have to pay $20,000 out of my pocket, and I'm afraid to lose this entire amount if I fail.

When confronted with such a decision, the thought comes to mind: what is the worst thing that can happen to me due to this decision? Well, I can lose $20,000. Could anything worse happen to me? Yes, many things are worse. For example, if we take an extreme case, if I get sentenced to death for some reason… but wait a minute – I was already sentenced to death. That happened the day I was born. I don't know when the judgment will be carried out, but it was already given. It cannot be appealed or evaded.

On further contemplation, another thought may come up: who promises me that I will still be alive on this date next year? Nobody. I may even not be among the living in a few more hours. Things like that have already happened. Even if statistically I'm supposed to live many more years, we all know how good statistics are for a person who was personally struck by lightning.

This may lead me to another thought: If tomorrow, God forbid, the doctor tells me that I have terminal cancer and have two more years to live in the best of cases, will I keep running my life the same way as I do today? Let's return to our example – would I save those $20,000 for a rainy day, or would I invest this amount right now? Would I invest the money without hesitation, to try and realize my idea? Maybe I would also reduce the time I dedicate to other endeavors and spend my last years with my family, or in fun, selfish activities, and not sacrifice my time for others?

Some may understand from this that it is important to try and live every day as if it is the last day of our lives. I do not really agree with this interpretation. We shouldn't take matters to extremes - again, due to statistics. Most chances are that this isn't the last day of your life (and if it is, too bad that you're spending it reading a book written for the most part to help you in the future. This is not a very smart choice, my friend!)

What I'm trying to say is that one shouldn't be too scared of risks. To make progress, one must dare to take a risk – not an extreme risk perhaps, but a certain measure of risk is necessary, as otherwise success would not knock on your door (though lottery winners might disagree with this).

I believe that most of our concerns and conservatism come from irrational fears. Think about this for a moment – this is absolutely illogical! Each and every one of you has been sentenced to death. This is a certain, absolute verdict. There is no way to appeal it or to evade its execution. For most of us, unfortunately, this verdict will also be executed painfully, slowly and humiliatingly. Old age, exhaustion, disease, the loss of dignity and control of body and mind, disgrace and abasement… in short – a true torture. Death by torture. Worse than this – an identical verdict, perhaps even more atrocious, was also issued against our loved ones: our friends and family members – our children, grandchildren and great grandchildren, and the great grandchildren of our great grandchildren.

We live in acceptance of this horrible piece of news without fearing its consequences in our day-to-day lives (maybe we repress, maybe we simply try not to think about it), but we don't use a similar mechanism in other matters. We are afraid to demand the promotion that we deserve at work, afraid to quit our job and start on a new road, afraid to learn something new or move to a new apartment, and out of fear, we avoid investing in ourselves or believing in ourselves. At the same time, we live in carefree complacency with the death sentence awaiting us.

This is so absurd! Think of what we have to face: the knowledge of our own certain death, the fact that our loved ones will also die, the terminal diseases and old age (which some may also call a terminal disease) in our horizon. This is all fine with us, but facing a simple business risk? That's already too much!

Another important point is related to the title I chose for this chapter. All rivers flow to the sea and all of us advance to our end. At the end we will all turn to dust and ashes, zero, nought, no matter what we have done in our lives. Can you name the richest man in Nineveh, the capital of Assyria, which was the strongest empire in the ancient world? Can you name the most brilliant scientist in Tokugawa's court? And who was the prettiest woman in the Ottoman Empire?

Well, from such a great historical distance, the richest man in Assyria and the most wretched beggar in town are the same. The prettiest woman in Constantinople and the ugliest and most repulsive woman in town, the brilliant Japanese scientist and the fool of the village or the court jester are quite the same. The highest and most elevated of men and the simplest and lowliest among them are very similar to one another, and even sadder – they are both almost genetically identical to a common chimpanzee.

In short, there is no reason to take life too seriously. It's better to live it out, and one should dare and not allow others to make you think that you are less worthy than they are, or that you do not deserve more. Looking at the broad picture – if person X "deserves" something, there is no reason that person Y shouldn't have it as well. We all have our human limitations and it's important to overcome them – otherwise success (and financial success is only one type of success) will not come, and also salvation will dally.

 ## THE TOOLBOX FOR CHAPTER THREE – ACCEPTING DEATH AS PART OF LIFE

Take everything in realistic proportions. So you lost money on your venture – but at least you tried. You dared. You lived. And you will be able to try again. At the end of the day, persistence and daring are key to victory, more than any other quality.

Always think about death. Compare any risk that you consider taking to the risk that will materialize in any case – the risk of you dying at a certain stage. Think how your decision would be influenced by the knowledge that you only have two more years to live. When you put the risk in these proportions, the demon is not all that bad.

It is very depressing to write this, but human life is sad by its nature. We are sentenced to death, and the life that awaits us until that point is strewn with suffering and hardship. At the end of the day we are small, puny and bereft of meaning. The lucky people among us, the wise ones, only understand their existential lack of significance with greater clarity.

And I say – we have already received all of these blows. Why give ourselves further blows? Why shouldn't you believe in yourself? Why should you let yourself be stopped by risks?

This is similar (and I apologize in advance for making this comparison) to a condemned man who has no right to appeal, and who is now afraid to stab and injure his cellmate, who had stolen from him the more comfortable mattress, because he may receive several more prison years - or who is afraid to steal a juicy mango from the prison cafeteria because he may spend there a few more months.

My approach is: you already got the death sentence? It's final? So at least be human beings, not mice. So long as your sentence is not carried out, sleep like a human being in your cell (even if this means receiving several more years in prison, which are insignificant for you, as we said above), and of course have juicy mango every day (and we provide no further explanations).

CHAPTER 4

The Importance of a First Impression

With regard to creating a positive first impression, most of us think about our looks: the garments, the body language, the hand movements, the eye contact, the smile. Even furrowing our brows. Some people make a living precisely out of this need that we have, to create a good impression – those in the fields of aesthetics and plastic surgery, style and clothing consultancy and those who teach others to control interpersonal interactions, in order to improve the chances of success in various situations. People usually go through these various training programs in order to prepare, as candidates, for interviews that lead to desirable jobs.

If you were once told that the first impression is a very important matter – forget it. It's total nonsense. Generally, especially in business situations, the first impression is not an important matter. It is actually **the most significant and most important – sometimes**

the only matter that will determine whether you do well or fail.

In this chapter, I will try to illustrate how complex a first impression is – much more than the "grocery list" mentioned above, even if you complement it with several other key ingredients, such as humor. The items in the list are indeed critical, but are definitely not the whole story.

The conclusions brought in this chapter may appear trivial, but under the surface (if you read closely you may well notice this), the contents of this chapter are perhaps among the most complex and revolutionary in the book. The successful application of the principles brought here will already take you halfway to success.

I chose to open this chapter with the famous sentence out of "Epistolae ad Lucilium" by Seneca, to emphasize an important element in creating a first impression – a person's lineage.

I don't see it as important, whether the lineage is actual or pretended, only meant to create the necessary first impression. So long as it is there – lineage will count heavily in creating a first impression.

I will illustrate this with a few simple examples.

Let's say that you're invited to the annual, multi-participant dinner of a professional association, in which you are a member. You obviously expect, beyond obviously enjoying the event, the food and the drinks, to also meet people of your own field, with whom you may be able to do business. Such encounters are fertile ground for business success and for creating useful contacts, for the present and the future. The word "networking" has long since stopped being a bad word, as such acquaintances are invaluable.

Let us return to the annual dinner, with your permission. During the evening you meet four different types. Let us assume that they are all the same age, with a similar physical appearance and similar mannerisms. All of them have an occupation that is related to yours, conduct activities abroad and impress you to the same extent.

Here they are, all four of them, and I hope that these examples may speak for themselves:

The first is a foreign citizen from a European country. You look at the name tag next to his chair and find that he is a nobleman – a baron. The second is a local businessman, whose social standing appears to resemble your own, and just like you, he does not know many of the attendees. The third is a company CEO in your own field, and he is seated at the "dignitaries' table" – next to the guest of honor, who is a government minister, and two seats away from the guest of honor – the mayor of a large foreign city. The fourth is a local businessman who appears to know almost everyone in the hall and stops to chat with dozens and dozens of them.

Out of these four people, in whom will you invest the greatest efforts? Who will interest you more? Assuming that your time is limited, who of them, in your opinion, has the potential of bringing you greater benefits?

Most of you may well say that the local businessman, who is similar to you, is the least interesting of the four. Pay close attention – you have something in common with the entire group. You all sit at the same dinner held by the same association, and are more or less related to the same field. But these are only appearances. It is the person who is most like you, whose background is most similar to yours – the person with whom it would seemingly be the easiest to develop a conversation and perhaps become good friends – who interests you the least. You might even see him as a potential competitor.

The thing is that people, even when they love themselves dearly, are more interested in 'the other.' You know yourself already, and you cannot expect too many surprises with someone like you. There is no special interest or thrill in meeting people who resemble you.

The foreign baron, for instance, inspires immediate interest. Why? Because he's foreign and an aristocrat. Our brain automatically relates nobility with the enchanted world that we knew in legends that we heard as children – legendary riches, palaces, pomp, success and power. These are no longer relevant nowadays, and it is possible that most of the attendees are more successful, richer, smarter and even more interesting than the baron. This does not alter the fact that even the wisest and the most high-quality people in the hall will be interested in the baron – the title affords him a significant advantage. If we assume that someone announces every person who enters the hall, it is clear that any title added before a person's name, who enters the room, will immediately generate great interest and that the audience will examine him more closely. The title may also be relevant to the event – for example, attorney, professor, minister or parliament member – but it seems that the "baron" title will stand out in any forum.

The local businessman who holds conversations with everybody, will also win many points, thanks to the impression that he creates, as a thoroughly networked individual, who knows most of the attendees. Perhaps he only knows them very superficially. Perhaps they actually loathe him and would never collaborate with him in any way, and he may have perhaps shown himself in other circumstances as being an unreliable person, a crook, a fraudster. Nevertheless, a stranger in the group, whose entire interaction with this local businessman was limited to several seconds or minutes in a single evening, may get a completely different first impression.

Last but not least – the person seated at the dignitaries' table. He will also appear as an interesting, networked individual – he sits next to the celebrities of the evening. These people represent power, and therefore, without the least effort on his part, he is seen as having the same qualities and enjoying the right connections. Nevertheless, he may well have earned his place at the dignitaries' table with a donation that he gave to the organizers of the event.

I was personally present at such an event. A person was sitting there, who had paid (as I later learned) the amount of $2,000 (not a tiny amount, but certainly not astronomical) in support of the event. After that, for the entire evening he enjoyed the company of several senior officials in the economy and leaders of the business sector, and was courted by dozens of the attendees of that event. His yield on the investment was worth hundreds of thousands of dollars. New business opportunities came his way – a smashing success in building his image, such as he would never get from any advertising campaign and/or out of any actual business achievement. At the beginning of the evening he had no access to opportunities and no personal acquaintance with the senior officials. By the end of the evening, not only had he enjoyed opportunities galore, but he was now widely seen by people as being a person thoroughly acquainted with the senior leaders in the economy… all this, as we said above, at a tiny cost, compared to the yield.

Indeed, in the beginning of the evening he created a pretended, fake lineage – but the impression generated was real. Therefore, after a short while the lineage also became factual, and the impression was now based on reality – not on a half-truth or a lie. In this way, thanks to a little "push," something real, well-founded and true was created.

An important point that one should always remember, is that there is no way to escape a first impression that has already been created. Once created it is there, and even years of effort (this is no exaggeration!) will not suffice to repair the damage caused. The human brain catalogues people and associates them with sensations and memories. One may compare this to a tree. If the first memory generated (the first impression) is "rude, arrogant and stupid" – this will become the root of the tree, and so it will remain planted forever. Whenever you think about that person, it is the memory of the first impression that he left you with, that will come to mind. Even if you get to know each other for years and that person consistently shows wisdom, manners and humility – you will not be convinced and won't change your mind so quickly. A single misstep – for example, that one day when he acts nervously and without patience – will immediately bring up that first memory, in which he was catalogued as rude and stupid.

This also works the other way: a person who initially appears to you as positive and smart, polite and kind will have to contradict that first impression consistently and over a long period, for you to change your mind about him.

It seems that our reliance upon the first impression is ingrained in us for evolutionary reasons – for survival: it allows us to make high-quality, quick decisions while wasting minimal resources.

Another important point comes from the field of military tactics. One of its most important principles is "know the enemy," and an important ingredient in applying this principle is the attempt to adapt to the enemy's way of thinking, in order to anticipate his actions and reactions. When striving to create the desired first impression, your enemy is not really an enemy – but you envision a clear objective for victory. Always remember that you are versatile – you have a great variety of characteristics and qualities. In certain situations, we must bring to the fore a certain aspect of our personality and suppress the part that may harm us. Try to understand what is the "enemy's" assumption. Are you in a job interview? Try to think, what kind of person are they looking for? What will turn them on, what will give them the best impression? Are you in a business meeting? Think about the same thing exactly – and of course, what not to do or say – under which circumstances, in your view, will the negotiations blow up or lead to an impasse?

To create a positive first impression, one should approach the person, or the people (sometimes audience) in front of you – and usually the costs are negligible.

And we shouldn't conclude this chapter without a few words on beauty and personal care.

It is sad, but nevertheless proven by studies, that good-looking people are more successful than ugly ones. This statement is clearly related to the issue of the first impression. A company CEO will prefer a handsome, impressive salesman over a hunchbacked, strange salesman – even where the hunchback is tenfold better than the handsome salesman in his skills and abilities.

Natural beauty is something that people are born with. There is not much a person can do about it. Characteristics such as height, body structure, hair and eye color were already engraved in our genetic structure. Nowadays, one may repair some of these details in extreme cases. At times, plastic surgery is definitely called for – not only in order to make the patient feel better and improve his self-esteem, but also in order to improve the way society regards him. Sometimes, the removal of a single serious defect through surgical intervention may completely transform a person's entire life and economic potential. Quite often the change actually results from improved self-esteem, not necessarily from the way society treats him before and after the intervention.

Personal care is quite another matter, though. Notice that the people who star in Forbes' list of the world's richest persons are not especially good-looking… but most of them are well groomed. Do you have physical defects? Try to conceal them and pay attention to what you wear. Make sure your clothes are clean and fragrant smelling, behave properly, and make-up may also come in handy.

Many people are rather ugly, but very charismatic. They compensate for their ugliness with their personality (or the personality that they project outwards), complemented with a small dose of personal care. Sometimes they are seen as more attractive (even sexually) than other people, who look a hundred times better.

In summary, if you are concerned that you may not be attractive and that your outward appearance may significantly impede your progress – go online and see what the wealthiest people of the world look like. You may derive great encouragement from what you see. The most important conclusion is to employ good personal care and physical discipline, watch your behavior and your language. Right, and also to not fear the surgeon's scalpel when you feel that this will significantly contribute to the overall first impression that you create.

Perhaps to illustrate this last point, all over the world, TV shows have popped up as mushrooms after the rain, showing how an unattractive person may become quite a stunning person with a few simple steps. When you watch such a show, you see people (usually women) that you would never look again at, had you run into them in the street – who after a short while – hours, days or a few weeks –become the most attractive and outstanding person on the street, only through the outward first impression, without the advantages of a compelling personality.

THE TOOLBOX FOR CHAPTER FOUR – THE IMPORTANCE OF A FIRST IMPRESSION

The first impression may be the most critical element in your success.

In many situations, all of those advices such as "behave the way you are and it will come out all right" are simply utter nonsense. In critical junctures in life, it is better to plan the necessary changes for a good first impression, in the same way one prepares for a military operation, including the principle of "know the enemy." Try to think what the other party would think – the one you wish to impress.

It is always important to employ good personal care: a good physical condition, cleanliness, personal hygiene and appropriate, well-fitting clothes, plus some kind of personal touch – a unique item such as an impressive watch. For women, that part is much simpler, due to the greater variety of choices in garments, jewels and make-up.

A good first impression may also result from lineage – real or pretended. Sometimes a well-placed small investment (for example, a seat at the "dignitaries' table" or arriving to the event in a limousine or with a bodyguard, when you generally don't employ such measures) may become very significant.

It is even better to have the first impression come from other sources. If the person in front of you has already heard about you (good things…) before meeting you, it may only help – he will already have an initial associative idea about you, and every detail that strengthens this impression by your behavior, will absolutely seal that impression.

Last but not least – a recommendation that harks back to the opening phrase of this chapter: Each person can create a good, high-quality first impression, regardless of his starting point in life. You don't need to be a baron to do this. If you consistently emphasize the first impression that you want to create, there is a good chance that this impression will become reality. Your image of being successful will become actual success.

It is nevertheless important to remain consistent. Lack of consistency will lead you to failure, even to perdition. This does not contradict the idea of creating a different first impression with different people and in different situations – quite the opposite – but this kind of approach is quite demanding and requires that you maintain the standards that you have set for yourself. This applies to behavior, and also to the small details, such as the personal care issue. You must be consistent and apply self-discipline, and not let yourself become lazy or deteriorate.

CHAPTER 5

How Other People Will Make You Rich

If you've already come this far in our book, you probably understand already that it's impossible (or very hard at least) to become rich through work. The road to wealth (and not necessarily to happiness) is usually paved with other people, who work for you and generate available income for you.

This is a correct assumption when you're running a company of any kind, as it is actually other people (the employees) who work and generate income for the company, but only receive a smaller part of it for themselves. This is also a deal that benefits everybody (but as you will see later – the owners of the company benefit more, if they know how to manage and conduct themselves businesswise).

The employees receive wages, make a decent living and enjoy stability and a sure income also when the market is weak, when they're sick, when they are less productive or when they're simply having a bad day – but the owner of the company enjoys all of their talents and abilities, and benefits nicely from every day they come to work.

I can give an example from my own experience, relating to this matter. One of the services that my company provides is a monthly maintenance service in the field of data security. This is an important but rather simple service – a data security expert visits the client, checks all of the computers in the organization and makes sure that all of the data security tools (antivirus, firewall, updates) are operational and up to date. He tries to detect suspicious activity by checking the computers and studying the activity logs (i.e. the running documentation of everything that goes on over the web, that helps detect suspicious, unusual activity) of the data security tools.

The person we send to perform this inspection has to be a data security professional. He is generally paid about $40 per hour of work – not a paltry sum. His wages cost us $8,000 every month, or $96,000 every year.

Here's a little professional secret: we charge our clients at least $110 for a working hour of this type - a rather low fee for the market we operate in. For service by professionals of my own level (expertise and knowledge), one may even charge as much as $700 an hour. Anyone who hears this and understands that the ordinary employee only receives $40 an hour, immediately thinks that the profit percentages here are high (if the employee only receives $96,000 a year but the company makes $220,000 for his services, there is a profit of over $120,000 a year right there) – but this is not the case.

In employing this expert, one incurs a variety of incidental costs: taxes, which bite deeply into the profits, management and accounting costs, numerous insurance policies that the employer must purchase (also to cover omissions by the employees) and travel expenses. The employee also receives his wages when there's nowhere to send him (this is why it is important to try and find other productive activities for him, or to make sure that there is 100% work for each employee – hidden unemployment is one of the greatest problems in managing employees). Of course, there's the main cost – running a marketing and service lineup that finds clients, as well as a whole lineup intended to preserve them and make sure that they're happy. Very high costs are associated with obtaining the client and preserving him, and the profits made by the daily operations should also cover these.

So far I have written a lot but only said a little. One can finally say that the basic option is to work on one's own – for instance, as a data security expert (or an attorney, or a person with unique knowledge and ability in any other field) - and to provide all of the services personally, including marketing, sales and managing the business. In this case you will be limited (and that applies to the peak of phenomenal success – 100% clients and 100% work), let us say, to a wage of $110 an hour - $220,000 a year, in exchange for very hard work throughout the year. This income is of course greatly reduced after taxes and expenses – let us say, down to $80,000 a year. Even if you reach the uppermost income level and enter the range of $700 an hour, you will still not become rich out of this. Theoretically, your income can increase six fold, let us say to $500,000 a year, after deducting taxes and expenses.

With a different working model, you can retain a marketing

person in your enterprise, whose entire function is finding new clients and preserving the existing ones, as well as four data security experts, who will provide the services. Let us say that the marketing man "eats" all of the profits and revenues generated by 1.5 data security experts, who are employed full time, and that the activities of the company only require 3.5 experts, not four. Let us also say that the final profit we make on a data security expert, net of all expenses, is $40,000 a year. This means that after we employ the marketing expert and pay our expenses, including the expert's wages, the enterprise remains with the same annual profit - $80,000 a year (or $500,000 if we apply the high wages, as the case may be), and we still have one-half of a full-time job available (we employ four experts but only have work for 3.5 of them, as above): we may use the time of one of the data security experts in order to generate more activity or assets (for example, we may have him develop data security software, hoping that it may become productive property).

At the end of the day, your profit as the business owner is similar in both models (let's say, $80,000 a year in the first, simpler and more reasonable example), but there are some differences, which obviously work in favor of the second model (a business with employees).

In the second model, you almost do not have to do actual work. You work very little, and that little work you do is of a different type – it's management work. You only have to make sure that everything is all right and that the employees work well. This is all. You can use your spare time to generate more income and more ideas, maybe even other business or other work (for example, I worked for quite a while as an employee, while also managing my business, enjoying the best of both worlds).

When applying the second model, you also contribute to society – you feed six families, not only your own. In addition, the second model gives you greater chances for expansion and stability. Even the impression you create with your clients is different. Some clients (especially larger entities) would not work with a single person, but only with a bigger operation. The second model has a further advantage: it depends upon you to a much lesser extent. Even if you are sick or depressive, or if you underwent a horrible accident, the business keeps operating and generating income. If you built your business the right way, your presence will not be necessary for it to function properly. Of course, there are also disadvantages, but I feel that they are negligible if you run your business properly. The main disadvantage is that you may create an increasing burden of "cash burning," which in turn requires you to increase your turnover and revenues, compared to the model of single-handed work. There is a constant need to cover the recurring expenses of the operation, that now also include the burden of additional salaries - often the most significant element in the entire expenses column, certainly in high-tech professions.

It may well be that the most important advantage of the second model – beyond those already mentioned – is that it has its own value. A ten-year-old company that has its own clients, contracts and reputation, and that consistently makes $80,000 a year in profits, may easily be sold to another person as a going concern – even for $800,000. Companies have value. They appreciate, as an asset. When you work alone, the orders of magnitude are different, and your work will probably never consolidate into an asset.

So far, we have spoken about relying on other people as income-generating employees, but this attitude also applies to other subjects. When you write a book (for example, on ways to become wealthy), you are confident that you are speaking wise words and that people will agree to dedicate a tiny portion of their income to purchasing the book. When many such people exist, the tiny amounts received from each one of them will accumulate into significant profits for you.

In a small community with 1,000 people, out of whom, let us say, one hundred people are your enthusiastic readers (this is huge – 10% of the entire population), it is obviously unadvisable to write books as a profession. Investing a year of work in writing a book, and then investing in having it published, will not pay when the target audience only numbers 100 potential buyers – even if we assume that 400 more buyers will purchase the book in the following years – unless the book is sold at an especially high (and unrealistic) price. In this case we may have the chicken and egg situation: the price will skyrocket and we will finally remain with ten buyers, not a hundred… one can always play a little with the income expectancy by changing the price (this is an art in its own right – how to price a service or a product, in order to reach the maximum profit), but the changes are not necessarily dramatic. This is even more the case if you have "kept the book in the drawer" for several years, as I did with this book…

This holds true for any other field, in which you invest in generating an asset and trust that others will use it in the future for a fee. Investment in a patent is the classical example, and also in anything defined as intellectual property (books, films, music and so on). Even the purchase of a tangible asset such as real estate, ultimately depends upon other people (tenants or buyers).

But let us return to the model, in which people are your

employees, who generate the income for you. This is the classical model for becoming wealthy. One of the most important points in any organization is identifying capable individuals. Some people may tell me that in a waste disposal organization, one does not have to find geniuses, unlike the high-tech industry. I beg to differ. As an owner of a waste disposal business, you would want geniuses to work for you. Certainly. I will explain to anyone who now raises a brow (or two) what I mean.

Indeed, in the high-tech industry, even the employees with the most basic skillset should be high-quality (and earn accordingly, which is of course a significant disadvantage for the owner of the company), **but the managers and marketing personnel in the waste disposal company should be quite as high-quality**. The waste disposal company will require high-quality management – perhaps of an even higher standard than is necessary in the high-tech company. Both because the employees in this field are tougher to manage, precisely because they come from a more problematic social stratum, and as concerns daily operations such as bidding on tenders, developing connections with local authorities, working with suppliers and with the state authorities, and marketing. The challenges are similar and sometimes tougher, especially as there is no unique product or patent here, and it is relatively easy to compete in a business of this type. One does not require great sophistication to purchase a waste-disposal truck and drive it, but one must be very sophisticated indeed, to run a successful business in this field and win the relevant tenders.

Better people than I have said this: if you want to become rich, you must know how to find geniuses, employ them and keep them close to you as long as possible. You do not have to be a genius yourself, to enjoy the fruit of genius (even though, of course, it won't harm you). Many geniuses and good managers are quite unfit to be business owners. They lack the necessary qualities, but they are highly fit to be especially productive employees.

Many people fear taking the step of becoming independent and starting a business. Do they not have economic security as employees? (Sometimes this is an illusion, but I will not expand on this here.) In order to detach oneself from this security, one needs nerves of steel. But if you want to become wealthy, you must be capable of withstanding pressures and persisting, be willing to take risks and dare to cut of dependency upon others. Sometimes, the people you rely upon collapse – see for example the Enron Company or the Israeli Bank of Commerce – and then your world might instantly turn to chaos. It is only at that point that you find that your sense of security in working in a stable place was nothing but illusion, and that you were actually dependent upon others, over whose actions, behavior or condition you had no actual control.

As an entrepreneur, you must find reliable, motivated and highly capable people, and of course high-quality professionals, whose combined qualities will ensure that you can sleep well at night, when you go on a ninety-day holiday in the Caribbean Islands. With the right employees, you will discover when you come back, that without you being involved (or with minimal involvement) not only was the business run in model fashion, it even expanded and grew in your absence.

Think for a moment about most of the successful companies that you know, especially the bigger ones among them. Is the CEO involved in day-to-day activities? Apparently not. Middle management runs the company, along with the lower echelons. They are the ones who bring new ideas and initiatives. They are those who do the work!

The senior managers (especially the CEO) perform a more representative role. Of course, they keep the machine functioning properly and their decisions only apply to the macro level. Even if we sometimes see a CEO who works very hard, generally the shareholders "rest on their laurels." They made the initial investment or took the initial risk, such as pouring good money into a new outfit, and when the business establishes itself they make profits without further investments. They have actually created an asset – human and non-human at the same time.

By the way, a few small and non-trivial tips for locating high-quality individuals:

Beyond the regular, proven methods, such as studying CVs, interviews, tests and perhaps most importantly – personal impression (if you're good at that and you're also an entrepreneur, your success is almost guaranteed), I would put some stress on considering capabilities acquired in childhood.

What do I mean? For example, it is advisable to examine the language skills of the person in front of you. In my view, one should mainly examine their mother tongue, not languages acquired in later years. One of the fundamental skills acquired in the early stages of life is the command of language. Vocabulary, pronunciation, the way one creates sentences, the way one thinks with words – these mostly form during our first years. These years are also responsible for most of our skills and for our way of thinking. A rich language generally attests to being educated in a good, high-quality home, to curiosity and to a great amount of reading from an early age. It generally says very good things about the person in front of you. Of course, I do not categorically condemn people, whose language is dull, but from my experience, this is one of the best indicators of human quality. I have met many brilliant people, extraordinarily successful and original thinkers, who came from a very bad economic background, but who still grew up in a well-cultured home. Their parents invested in them when they were children, and their rich language attests to this.

By the way, I always prefer high-quality people who come from a problematic background. It is much easier to be high-quality and successful when you have grown up in a home without any objective difficulties, enjoy good education and have private tutors. It is harder to succeed in a home with limited economic possibilities, where you have only received a basic education and your success mainly depends on you. Therefore, if you meet a successful and well-educated individual who comes from a bad background, it is generally evidence of a tough, determined character, and there is a good chance that you can rely upon him at times of crisis. The tough background will also guarantee that he will treat crises coolly, without losing his nerve.

And here's my little tip – examine qualities that are influenced by the childhood of the person in front of you. Finally, the background in which we grew and were raised has a great influence over the person we grow up to be. By the way, this tip does not only concern the selection of good employees, but also the rearing of children. What you sow is what you will reap. With good education and personal sacrifice, you can establish the success of your children.

I did not grow up in a wealthy home, but our home was still full of books and encyclopedias. At the age of two I already had a personal computer (manufactured by Apple, of all companies – an Apple IIc, the cradle of home computers), despite its high cost, and much was invested in me. I learned skills and acquired great knowledge as a child, while building a rich inner world and assimilating values, social manners and a great deal of culture.

The investment in a child is immense, economically and emotionally. It requires a great portion of a parent's time. This is not a simple challenge for a family, but this is their future. If we don't invest here, when will we invest? I hope that the greatest success I ever have will be in raising my daughters to be better and more high-quality than I am. Of course, I will also be happy if they become financially successful, but this is not the most important parameter. In my opinion, the health of our children is more important than anything else, and after that comes their quality as human beings. Regarding financial success – it is always nice to have more (there are quite a number of Jewish sayings on this subject), but experience shows that if there's no choice, one may make do with a single financially successful individual in a family…

THE TOOLBOX FOR CHAPTER FIVE – HOW OTHER PEOPLE WILL MAKE YOU RICH

To become wealthy, you must learn to rely upon other people. Only they will make you rich. It is important to become proficient in reading people – to know who is professional and who is reliable, who you can get along with in the long run, who is a genius or a bright person and who has a brilliant future. Try to become proficient in identifying human strengths and weaknesses. Isolation from human society will not help you. On the other hand, contact with as many people as possible will increase your chances to become wealthy.

To be wealthy without working, one needs assets. If you were not born with assets, you will have to produce them. It is a bit difficult to generate real estate, because first of all you have to purchase an expensive property, but to create a company or a business based on human capital, you need no original capital. A company is an asset and so are employees. Once the wheels start moving without you, know that you're on the right road.

It is indeed very scary, not to be an employee. It is even scarier to count on other people (which is why most independent workers work on their own, or with very few employees. It is much easier for a person to trust himself than a hired manager), but one needs to let go in this sense, in order to become wealthy. If you cannot trust others and do not know how to make them work, being wealthy probably doesn't suit you.

CHAPTER 6

Building a Successful Image
with Practical Tools

As we wrote in earlier chapters, creating a successful image is a critical element in obtaining actual success. Once one actually becomes successful, it is not too difficult to obtain and present a successful image – even though one must still preserve it, cultivate it and take care of it from time to time.

By way of example, it is clear to all of us that a person who projects an image of failure will not inspire others to join him in various ventures. It is similarly clear that a silent, sullen and gloomy person will not be capable of sparking enthusiasm in others and sweeping them off their feet. A filthy, dirty individual will not be able to represent a company that sells personal care and hygiene products (unless he stars in a "before and after" campaign, showing the transformation he underwent and the gap between the existing and the desired).

I will make a much stronger statement: people believe what they want to believe.

"Seeing is believing," goes the maxim – one must see in order to believe. A person only believes what he sees and what is empirically proven to him – but I tend to believe that for most of us it is exactly the other way – "believing is seeing." When we expect to see something, our brain distorts reality to match our expectations. Our brain makes us believe that we have, indeed, seen that which we expected to see, and only strengthens our distorted concept of reality. This is why the image is the most critical element.

A few examples will illustrate this:

First, let us take an esteemed professor, a Nobel Prize winner, who is invited to lecture to an audience of young students. His image is of a true genius in his field, and his lecture is expected to be enthralling. As it happens, the subject of the lecture is boring, totally beyond the understanding of the audience. In addition, on that day the professor was hoarse and nervous, and his lecture was atrocious in every sense. By previous experience, we can tell that it's quite possible that many people in the audience will still praise the professor and his lecture, enjoy it and even tell their friends and acquaintances about it, if only because of the high expectations that they had of that person and his lecture. Had one of their friends delivered that same lecture exactly, they would tag him as a "boring idiot," but here they were heavily impressed by the image.

The second example may be better. Scientists from the University College in London, led by Professor Zhaoping, have examined this issue scientifically, from a mathematical standpoint. They wanted to know whether our beliefs derive from what we actually see and perceive, or is it that our beliefs, together with earlier "background noise," could overshadow what we actually see and even convince us that we have seen something quite different. In their experiments, the researchers managed to make people see and perceive things that did not exist at all, and to ignore things that they have seen clearly – all based on their beliefs, various "background noises" and suitable preparation. When a subject expected to see something and something else happened, his brain "aligned" itself automatically according to his expectations, ignoring the actual scene. Moreover – after the fact he "remembered" that the expected scenario had occurred, not the actual event, and was willing to attest to that with complete faith!

The percentage of people, whose brain did not "align" itself according to expectations and who have actually observed reality, was negligent to non-existent in most experiments. It was proven beyond any doubt that such people were the outliers in the population.

By the way, this phenomenon explains how come many magic and illusion shows are so successful – but I want to deliver a deeper message. Each of us has expectations, beliefs and opinions on various subjects. When something happens that confirms our beliefs, we tend to embrace it with a bear hug, but when something happens that contradicts them, we will dismiss it right away and sometimes even ignore it altogether, as if it never existed.

This also applies to our image in the eyes of others. If we manage to create a positive image prior to any real interaction with us, when such interaction actually takes place, our chances to succeed are probably much higher already, and the image that we have created may well overcome significant evidence to the contrary.

You may call it "threepenny psychology," but I call it "million-dollar psychology."

The best way to create an image is to have a conversation started about us, through sources that are not related to us, which is held without our participation. The simplest way to do this is perhaps through the media. A newspaper article, a radio or a TV show, even an Internet blog or information from social networks, would achieve this goal.

Let us take, for example, the legendary investor Warren Buffett. I'm sure that many of you have heard about him. One thing is certain, the great majority among you has never met Buffett personally and never had the occasion to talk with him. Your knowledge mostly comes from information published about him in the media. For the benefit of those of you who have never heard of him, I will only say that this is one of the biggest investors in the world, one of the richest people on Earth, who has been obtaining huge yields on his investments for over thirty years, beating the markets time after time, by using relatively simple, conservative models. He recognizes opportunities in the market and pounces on them. He has a proven record of success for decades. He is said to be a very nice and charismatic individual.

And why am I presenting this nice guy?

Well, certainly not by accident. To illustrate the power of the media and its tools, I will take a practical example, in which I pit myself against Warren Buffett. Let us say that during the last fifteen years of your life you have saved a significant amount of money, which you hold very dear. Perhaps you are even counting on it for your later years. One day, you meet two people – me, and Warren Buffett. Neither of us usually makes business proposals to people, certainly not to someone we have just met on the street by sheer accident – but we both like you, and we both suggest that you join us in a venture. We claim that we have an idea for a great innovative product, and what we suggest to you (because we have taken a great liking to you, not because we need your money, God forbid!) is very simple: we will help in the business development of the idea, and you will venture the whole amount of money that you have been saving over the last fifteen years. You listen to my idea – and it really sounds revolutionary to you, with great potential. Warren's idea, on the other hand (I'm sorry, Warren – nothing personal, just a hypothetical example), sounds rather grey, boring and grim. You don't really believe in its success.

My question is: which one of us will receive your money?

As sad as this may be, my chance of getting this investment from you is close to zero. You have probably never heard about me, and those people you will turn to for advice have also probably never heard about me. On the other hand, **Warren Buffett?** The very fact that such a well-known person, with such a successful image, has proposed something to you is so rare – more or less like your chance of winning the lottery. You may even see yourself as a lottery winner already during your meeting with him. By the way, every year, that same Warren Buffett offers a dinner meeting with him at his favorite steak house in Omaha, Nebraska, for several hundreds of thousands of dollars (which he then donates to charity). Your meeting with me, as impressive as it may be, will not give you such a feeling of euphoria, and doubts will linger in the back of your mind.

If you ask acquaintances, friends or experts for advice, obviously all of them (including your own "gut feeling") will tell you to board that train (the deal with Warren), even if his idea seems awful to you. Hasn't Warren already proven (over more than thirty years) that he can recognize the best ideas, those that others miss? And you are among the "others" and do not have Warren Buffett's sharp business sense – otherwise you would have been that old billionaire, that so many people wish they could meet.

Even if you now conduct an in-depth study that ultimately shows that over the last few years, the performances of my own investments were extraordinary even by Warren Buffett's own standards, and if after examining a few of his last investments you find failures, reverses and less brilliant decisions than he used to make, you will still not allow the facts to confuse you. Neither you nor your friends know me, while Warren is a well-known billionaire who is a star both in the media and in literature and who consistently wins the praises of most financial commentators (the majority of whom, surprisingly, are not rich people) on every occasion. Some of them even see him as a role model, a financial idol of sorts, and "pray" to him every week, much more often than they pray to their own God in the synagogue, the church, the temple or the mosque.

But wait a minute… you were very impressed by my idea, while his appeared appalling. You strongly felt that my proposal was good and that his was horrible, and yet you are likely to dismiss this. Moreover – when I present the proposal to you, many of you will be very reluctant to risk such a great amount of money, that was earned through such great efforts over so many years. Only the most adventurerous among you will be thrilled. You may even prefer to let go of the opportunity to become rich and hold on to what you already have, in the spirit of that wise maxim "a bird in the hand is worth two in the bush." But if Warren Buffett contacts you, I'm sure that many of the most conservative among you, those who would not even dare to think of a scenario in which they would even touch that money, will become the most daring adventurers.

Is it Warren's character? His leadership? His charisma? His values? The cultural kinship he has with you? I strongly doubt it. He may well be a total stranger to you, quite a strange individual, who does not speak your language, has no ties to your culture and heritage, and you never had the time to get to know him well or to seriously study his proposal. And yet, many of you will be willing to "jump into the deep end" and risk fifteen years of savings and hard labor, **just because of his image**, and very surprisingly – it is quite likely that **the image** will become reality. In my estimate, Warren owes at least 60% - 70% of his success to the image he has built. The positive image creates actual success, which may well be the great secret of his success.

You have read my words and you think that I may be bitter or angry. Some may even say 'whiny.' My idea was so good and Warren's was so bad, and you still decided to entrust your money to him, without a second thought, quite irrationally.

But you know what? This is not my point.

I think that may be the right thing to do, to some extent. Warren's image is so good, that he can sell a product or find more investors even when the product is very bad. The very fact of you having joined him, already increases your chances to succeed and is already a minor success in its own right! Other clients and potential investors who hear about this venture will also employ the same (not necessarily rational) reasoning.

Please note – I didn't claim that Warren was going to invest any of his own money. I didn't mention a possibility of him using his connections or any advantages that his great fortune affords him. The main difference between the offers is the image. It is very likely that even in the real world, a lame, inferior idea (from your perspective) that benefits from Warren Buffett's image will prevail over a brilliant, innovative idea, in which you believe with all of your heart, but which lacks the backing of such an image.

Of course, it's possible that you didn't opt to harness the power of the image, but in that case, I'm sure that it was not an easy decision to make. The fact that you find it hard to decide strengthens my argument about the importance of an image. **It is not simple to create an image, but once it is created – it is very hard to break – a very extreme and unusual sequence of events is required.**

This leads me to the second, last and simplest part of this chapter. I mentioned the steps for creating a personal image with the help of friends, personal experiences and perhaps most importantly – data distribution tools, and first and foremost among them – the written and electronic media. Building an image is a hard task. A very hard task. It may require years.

But the last part of this chapter actually encourages you to use the simplest practical tool to create a successful image: **joining people who already have a good image.**

This is perhaps the most important lesson one can learn from the dilemma that I have presented here: the power of an image is so important, that joining people who have already earned the correct image may perhaps be the most critical step you can make in marketing your ideas and messages. If you manage to choose the right people, you will probably also earn a positive and lasting image, which will be influenced by the people with whom you associate.

THE TOOLBOX FOR CHAPTER SIX – BUILDING A SUCCESSFUL IMAGE WITH PRACTICAL TOOLS

A successful personal image is critically important. It is important to keep investing in it for years. Beware of extreme acts that may demolish your image.

Remember, sometimes the image is more important than the true nature – people choose to see what they want and expect to see. In order to make it, one should invest in one's image similar efforts as one invests in the other essential matters.

An important point: it is always better when the information sources that speak about you are objective, external and foreign to you. The distance neutralizes any possible influence you may have over the information, and makes it appear reliable. There are always opportunities to create a positive image through your own initiative – an image that will appear objective to the outside observer. Don't overlook them.

And perhaps the most important message in this chapter – it is very hard to create a positive image, especially an image of success. Find other people who are available to you in one way or another, and who already have a positive image of the kind you are looking for, and join them (and conversely, beware of people who have a negative image). Carry out your business ventures with them, even if you have to give up a significant percentage of the venture – sometimes even at the price of remaining "in the shadows" while the owner of the image stands in the front line and faces the public. The very fact of joining such people will contribute to your image in the long run, helping you to create a kind of "image-related brand" that will stand on its own feet. Of course, more importantly

– joining this person will help you achieve your short-term goals.

It is worthwhile (and very advisable) to pay for a successful image. It is more beneficial than many other actions that you pay for without blinking, and is sometimes much more significant than the core actions. A mediocre product with a positive image is much likelier to succeed than a superb product without an image, or with a negative image. Of course, a superb product may well generate its own positive image over time, but this is the point – over time. You will not live forever, and unless you intend to reach your image-related objectives only when you're ready to meet your maker (or after that) – perhaps you should take into consideration this little piece of advice.

CHAPTER 7

Sources of Livelihood on the Road to Wealth

You certainly remember that already at the beginning of this book I doubted that one could become wealthy through hard work. In this chapter I will explain more clearly what I meant.

Consider this: if you only rely upon normal work, you dramatically lower your chances to succeed. I am not trying to claim that you may avoid work. To make it, you will most likely have to work hard while also investing much in external ventures and in creating the assets that you will later use to propel yourself – all at the same time and possibly over many years (until you have enough assets and can do away with conventional work).

Many of you might say that what I am describing here – and throughout the entire book – is too demanding. Too tough. Much tougher than hard work.

An example will illustrate this: Two talented 25-year-old individuals are very capable in a certain profession and earn a very good living. For the sake of argument and to make it simpler for those who disagree with my approach, let us assume that both of them are fully capable of soundly establishing themselves in their jobs. They will not be fired and will never face unemployment at any stage of their career.

One of them gets by through hard work. Every day he comes to the office, returns home in the evening and earns his living from each day's toil. We already know that even if he makes great strides in his workplace, his chances of becoming wealthy that way are very minimal. Such things have happened, but as we already said – there are more lottery winners than rich employees, and in many professions it is not even an option. The glass ceiling and social norms tend to establish us comfortably within the middle class. When our man is tired, he rests. Every now and then he treats himself and his wife to some indulgence – an expensive piece of jewelry or a trip abroad. Sometimes he even "goes wild" and buys an apartment that he cannot afford, with the help of a large mortgage, or drives a new and expensive car (of course not a luxury car). You probably know many people who fit this exact profile. In Western countries they form a large portion of the population. People who can afford to live in an average house, keep average cars, enjoy a few little treats during the year and generally "live rather well," as our society defines this. Some will call this a bourgeois lifestyle, or "the American dream," but please note – many people live like this, but have quite different dreams. Many of them are unhappy – they are frustrated and bitter, and this makes you doubt: perhaps this life, into which we are pressured by society, is not quite the dream.

With your permission, let us return to the second individual. Just like his above colleague, he lives from hard work and holds a similar job. They both earn exactly the same – but when this second guy ends his working day he does not go back home, but dedicates his time and energy (whatever is left of it) to other ventures –his own business perhaps, or maybe patents, investments, real estate or any other field he may choose, that has a potential for generating assets and income. Whenever he has a few free moments, he does not spend them on the sofa, watching TV with a beer in hand. He does something, or at least thinks about what he needs to do to promote his additional private undertakings. He looks for opportunities. That extra money he acquires during the initial years will not be invested in treats. He makes fewer trips abroad, lives in a cheaper apartment, drives a simpler, older car, purchases the proper insurance policies and propels his free, available funds towards success.

Some will prefer the first person's lifestyle. His life is certainly more relaxed, with fewer worries and in the early stages of independent life, when you're younger, it may be more tempting and pleasant. This is of course a legitimate choice – but still a conscious choice (or perhaps unconscious, borne of sheer inertia) not to pursue financial success. And I say – if this is your choice, why did you buy this book? Out of pure curiosity?

The older you get, the more you understand that life doesn't really come in black or white, but in shades of grey. One may also choose a middle path, between those two types I described. This middle path involves a lesser degree of risk and effort – and therefore, of course, leads to lesser successes. It still promises higher chances of success than those enjoyed by the average person.

Later in this book, I will prove to you that $300 saved by a person aged 20 will grow almost six fold once he reaches the age of retirement, even with very conservative investments. It is possible to explain the greatest differences between the financial conditions people have by this datum alone.

Let us take our first individual and paint him "grey" by changing his behavior very slightly. We will only change two details: he will spend a little less on luxuries (jewels, travel abroad). I am not saying that he should totally abstain from them, but he will buy cheaper jewelry and do it less frequently, and make fewer trips abroad, to cheaper destinations.

Let us assume that this change in his behavior will save $300 for him every month. In addition, he will buy (or rent, it doesn't matter in this context) a cheaper and more cramped apartment and will still drive a car, but a cheaper, more economical model – and so save an additional $400 every month, perhaps. His total savings will now reach $700. This person still relaxes on his couch in front of the TV with his beer. He still spends time with his family, rather than troubling himself with more business or a second job. He does travel abroad and spoil his wife with jewels, but in reasonable measure. Of course, this comes at a price – he currently lives not quite as well as the first individual, but… he saves $700 a month, which will actually be worth six times more in the long run. He actually saves a future $4,200 every month. This is $50,000 a year. Let us say that he lives like this between ages 20 and 40 - for twenty years – and his savings already reach $1,000,000. By the way, in this context, many of us are misled by the lies we are flooded with through the media, such as "no savings plan is consistently profitable over time." As I will explain later, plans such as an index basket certificate, which follows the stocks included in the Tel Aviv 100 or in the S&P 500 in the US, or even making real estate purchases over a number of years, are proven ways to generate steady profits. In the long run, it is quite reasonable to assume that the investor will multiply his savings by a factor of six, without the need of any exceptional knowledge.

This fact is quite hard to digest for most people – but those who become wealthy understand it well: They are the ones who did not drive a slightly bigger or more expensive car, did not have an extra ten or twelve unnecessary square feet in their apartment and did not buy unneeded clothes (that have long since been thrown in the trash) or unnecessary jewelry (that today is worth less than the day it was bought). Nor did they spend a few more vacations abroad, that were slightly more expensive – and as a result of these activities ended up wasting one million dollars.

Our grey man, who chose the middle path and saved on luxuries, can now go abroad every month, over and over again, for years. He can also buy a different car for each day of the week, help his children buy apartments and even buy so much jewelry for his wife, that she will look like a Christmas tree – and he will still have extra money. All of this – at the cost of only slightly reducing his standard of living during his younger years.

Both the grey man and the first man lived in an apartment – the grey man simply lived in a smaller one. They both drove a car – the grey one simply drove a slightly cheaper car. They both went abroad – the grey one simply travelled a little less often, to closer and cheaper destinations. At the end of the day, his investment had already paid off well by age 40, and this man may now compensate himself and enjoy life six times as well as the first man.

The way I see it, this illustrates exactly the difference between short-term and long-term thinking.

By the way, when I express my opinion on this subject I run into some interesting objections – especially from those who say that one should live for the day, because any day may be the last one of your life, and who ever promised you that you will reach old age? Their main argument is: "You deny yourself pleasures today and actually delay your gratifications for tomorrow, when nobody promises you that there will even be a 'tomorrow.' Maybe you will deny yourself many things, but in the end never get to enjoy what you have saved."

I have several answers to this argument:

First of all, forty is not old age…

Secondly, I will send anyone who presents this argument back to the first chapter of this book, on insurance. If indeed our fears come true and you never reach old age, you will not only not lose – financially you may be the great winner.

Thirdly, statistics show that most of us will indeed make it to old age. It would not be so smart to assume that precisely you are the outlier with regard to these statistics. This is exactly the problem – the avoidance of long-term planning.

Fourthly, please notice that I never said that one should abstain and lead an austere life. You can spoil yourself. You can spend time abroad. It is even desirable to buy a house and keep a car, but all in the right measure. The differences in the standards of living between the saver and the waster are minor, but when soberly viewed over long time periods, the gap is huge. A slightly more moderate lifestyle today equals a huge difference in your lifestyle and financial capabilities tomorrow.

One last point. Please show this book, along with the examples I have presented, and even repeat these arguments to anyone who has already made these choices and lived past age fifty, for example. Ask him if he regrets the choices he has made.

THE TOOLBOX FOR CHAPTER SEVEN – SOURCES OF LIVELIHOOD ON THE ROAD TO WEALTH

It seems that there is no way for you to avoid working for a living for many years, on the road to wealth (and happiness?). There is no reason to flinch. This is natural, correct and dictated by reality.

Nevertheless, if you want to really make it, be ready to make sacrifices. Also this cannot be avoided.

If you want to increase your chances to succeed, there's a price to pay.

It is quite likely that your household, your income and most of your spare time as young people will be sacrificed and harnessed for these chances – at least for several years, and these are the best years of your life.

I want to stress this – it is not certain that these chances will ultimately materialize. It is not certain that you will succeed. I cannot guarantee such a thing to you. Nobody can. But if you do this, you can later say, know and feel that at least you had tried. On the other hand, if you do not do this – you have consciously chosen not to succeed, or have turned a blind eye. Of course, intermediate roads exist, which perhaps suit most people. See the main example I showed in this chapter, the one about the grey man. If you read between the lines you will see that an average Western family, that only "tightens its belt" for about twenty years and acts in a financially calculated manner, may become a (small) millionaire during this short time period, while at the same time not taking financial risks or making substantial sacrifices – and this can also happen even before the age of forty. Think about it.

"Miserum est tacere cogi quod cupias loqui."

"It is miserable to be forced to remain silent about what you wish to say."

Publilius Syrus, Sententiae

CHAPTER 8

Reporting to Seniors; Reports from Subordinates

I chose to open with an interesting maxim that I will discuss later in this chapter. Here I will actually start discussing another well-known maxim that I believe in with all of my heart, and which many of us use often: **"You did but failed to tell about it – so you didn't do!"**

This maxim is pure truth: as far as others are concerned, if they were not informed of an action done by X, they consider that X has never done it. The simplest example to illustrate this is at the workplace - especially a big workplace.

Generally, a direct manager gives various tasks to an employee and then makes sure that he performs them well. In the most usual cases, the only people who would know about the nature and quality of that employee's work are his colleagues and direct manager. The manager's manager, for example, is not necessarily aware of that employee's qualities. The senior executive is in contact with the junior manager every day, but he does not know that out of a five-man team that works under the junior manager, a single person is behind 60% of the production and 100% of the proposed improvements…

Generally, the junior manager would be in no hurry to offer these data, but would rather keep them to himself. He has no reason to give credit to the good employee. Sometimes it's quite the opposite – the manager may consider that this would lead to the promotion of the employee at his own expense. Promotion would be very good news for the employee, of course, but sometimes very bad news for his direct manager, who loses the most precious worker and thereby suffers a serious hit in his own production.

Apart from this, employees often take an initiative that goes beyond their expected function, thereby bringing great benefits to their workplace. If they don't tell the story, they deserve no credit for this as far as other employees are concerned, and nobody will relate the employee's positive action to the result. Apparently, the achievement will be unrelated to the employee who accomplished it. It will be as if the accomplishment "just happened," or even worse – another person will be credited.

It is important, already at an early stage in any workplace, to create a regular reporting interface that will allow you to establish contacts not only with your direct manager, but also with senior management or with parallel elements in the company. It is important to establish such connections wisely, not in a way that might appear subversive or "bypassing the chain of command."

This is especially easy to do nowadays, through electronic media

– for example, sending a wider-distribution email with a description of the business accomplishment. Do not write "thanks only to my hard work, the project was completed in half of the expected time." You may mention, for example "I'm happy to announce that the project was completed in half of the expected time." Now, all of the recipients will know to whom to give thanks that the project was completed early, and if anyone in senior management is interested in the specifics, you can always provide them.

In summary – it is very good to excel, to take the initiative, to work hard, to succeed – but it is just as important to create suitable public relations for the work you did. This takes time and one has to create suitable interfaces with superiors and to invest thought and effort in graphics and representation (for example, preparing attractive presentations).

The recommended rule of thumb for rapid promotion: you would normally have to invest 90% of your time in actual work and 10% of your time creating public relations for work that you have done and reported, also before and during the actual work – not only upon completion.

The conduct described so far has also another side – the executive.

As an executive, it is important that you create interfaces for routine reporting and follow-up with your employees, so that you may obtain a true, complete picture of the scene under your responsibility, while neutralizing (as far as possible) any biased reports. For example, you may have an employee who reports every last detail, but whose production is only mediocre, and another employee, a superb one, yet who is shy and modest and does not take credit for his accomplishments. As an executive, it is important that you know the actual situation and have access to the full information. Additionally, it is important that you give credit to the employees who did the actual work, in your communications with senior management.

Make sure that your employees understand that their opinions count and that they are invited to express themselves freely. Clarify to them that they have access (though limited, perhaps) to senior management. As an executive, it is in your interest to promote their careers and their interests. You should have their backs.

Remember – the success of your employees is your own success as an executive.

And this brings us back to the opening maxim of this chapter: **"It is miserable to be forced to remain silent about what you wish to say."** Do not make your employees miserable! Delegate. Involve them as much as possible in the decision-making processes, let them take the initiative and lead (according to their capabilities) subjects that they believe in and are motivated and passionate about. Most importantly – even as an executive, you still wear the employee's hat towards your own managers (unless you are the Company CEO, in which case you have to report to the shareholders, to the public and even to the media in a rather similar manner). Just like the average employee and even more so, you should take determined action to promote your own and your employees' public relations, making others aware of your accomplishments.

 ## THE TOOLBOX FOR CHAPTER EIGHT – REPORTING TO SENIORS; REPORTS FROM SUBORDINATES

Whatever you do, running a private business or working as an employee – make sure other people know about your achievements and successes. Create awareness of your qualities and of the hard work that you have done.

If you are an executive, create suitable interfaces with your employees, to get the true picture. Also encourage the shier among them to report to you routinely. Remember, an executive also wears the employee's hat in other forums.

Perhaps the simplest suggestion - remember that rule of thumb: dedicate at least 10% of your working hours to documentation, to reporting - and of course to public relations.

"Animus facit nobilem."   *"Your spirit makes you noble."*
Seneca, Epistolae ad Lucilium

CHAPTER 9

Social Skills, Connections, Networking and Rubbing Elbows with Nobility

A critical condition to success is having good social skills, or alternatively the ability to join forces with a person, or several individuals, who have first-class social skills and who will compensate for our own limitations and lead us to success.

I'm sure that many of you had a huge, phenomenal, outstanding idea at some point of your lives – but you have probably done nothing with it. Why? Think carefully: Do any of the following excuses sound like you?

If only I had enough money to invest in it…
If only I had the time to engage in it…
If only I had the technical ability necessary to realize it…
If only I had investors for it…

If only I managed to get exposure for it…

If only I had someone to share the risk with…

If only I knew whom to contact in order to promote this…

If only I knew how to market it…

If only it were possible to protect this idea from being copied or stolen…

One may think of many more excuses, but they are actually "sub-excuses," subordinate to those brought here. Finally, most of us shy away from risks, from making significant changes in our lives and from chasing our dreams. We usually lack the funds necessary to create a new venture, to say nothing of financial reserves that would allow us to go without income for several years. We haven't the slightest idea how to reach potential clients or to market the venture, and most of us also lack the technical ability needed to realize the idea. Something is certainly missing (so many sub-specializations exist in our era. Almost no field is left, in which one person can do everything – "a one-man crew"), and most importantly – we all suffer (in varying degrees) from paranoid fears of being defrauded, having our idea copied, being dispossessed of our idea or being exploited, in which case all goes to waste. This is exactly the point at which our social skills win the day, and with panache. Here one can certainly create and make it in "one-man show" mode.

If you spend time in the correct social circles, you may find people who will manage to bridge all of these gaps for you (probably in exchange for something, of course, but these are the ways of the world – it is better to share a glorious palace with five people than to be the exclusive owner of a miserable shack).

The classical example is recruiting investors: You have an idea that may yield tens of millions of dollars but have no money to start putting it into practice. Some other people have extra money that they would be very glad to see grow. For you, the amount you need is way beyond the horizon, but for them it's a trifle. If you only manage to get to know and befriend them, you're all set.

By the way, money can bridge many of the other gaps between idea and realization, so I believe that the most important step is finding financing sources. When you have the money, you can hire professional manpower to work in the venture that you will create, protect your idea by hiring patent attorneys and other suitable attorneys and even employ marketing, business development and sales personnel, each an expert in their own field.

Beyond obtaining financing, social ties have further advantages. First of all, you won't believe this – you can make new friends and enjoy human interaction. Usually, as you will enter social circles that are relevant to your occupation or to the field you wish to promote, you will meet talented people with similar interests and backgrounds to yours - a non-trivial bonus.

Another advantage is getting to know potential partners. Both senior and junior partners are beneficial. You may meet a person with similar background and skills to your own, whom you can trust. If your problem is not having enough time to develop this venture, you can work on that venture together with this person. Initially you wouldn't be taking any risks. You will be maintaining your lifestyle and developing the venture as a "hobby." A single person may be overloaded if he tries to start a venture, but when you are two or three, the chances of propelling your venture and bringing it to solvency definitely increase. Each of you (if you are three) will eliminate one-third of the risk incurred by the other two members. The venture will grow and develop without you risking significant capital or having to disrupt the lifestyle that you have become so used to.

Later, if the venture picks up and shows signs of success, you can start taking care of it on a full-time basis without any risk. If the venture fails, at least you know that you have tried and you can now go on to the next idea. Most importantly – you didn't suffer great damages, because you have found someone to share your risk with. The only disadvantage is, of course, having to share your success with others. But as I mentioned before – it is better to be one of the owners of a palace and to live in it with more people, than to live alone in a miserable, dilapidated shack.

Now, let us talk about nobility. It is certainly clear to you that nowadays, real nobility is all but extinct in the world, in the literal sense of the word. The nobility that still exists, even a high figure such as the queen of England, is not necessarily capable of helping you. Only few real noblemen (by lineage) are left in the world, such as the crown prince of Liechtenstein, Hans Adam II, who also owns the LGT fund.

The "nobility" that I am talking about here includes, for example, people from your own field who have already "made it." Are you a high-tech entrepreneur? The "stars" within that noble circle that concerns you would be other entrepreneurs who have already started companies and successfully sold them or offered them to the public. Are you an engineer or an architect? Look for other engineers and architects who have erected gigantic, unique projects – for example the Borg El Arab in Dubai. Do you own a clothing store? You will look for that noble circle that contains the entrepreneurs who have established international clothing retail chains, such as Zara. If you own a furniture store or factory, the (now late) founder of IKEA certainly belongs to the nobility in your field.

It is important to note – in many cases, a person who is part of that noble circle may be your competitor. He may try to trip you up, but one thing is sure: if he wants, he has the power of putting you on the road to success and to absolute independence. He already has the right connections and can help you with marketing, business development, raising capital and even goodwill and building your reputation.

On the other hand, you don't have to get his help directly. You can learn many things just by spending time with him. Call it "a modern apprentice." Sometimes all you need is a person who is in touch with your nobleman – a lawyer, a banker, a public relations person, etc. It is enough for you to have dinner with him once, and you are on the road to success.

THE TOOLBOX FOR CHAPTER NINE – SOCIAL SKILLS, CONNECTIONS, NETWORKING AND RUBBING ELBOWS WITH NOBILITY

The point I am trying to make in this chapter, which was hopefully well delivered, is the following: Just as you need other people (employees being the classical example) in order to really make it, it is necessary that you also weave a social network, which will serve you. You also need other people in order to succeed – they will fill in your inherent gaps and shortcomings.

It is important to invest considerable time in social affairs. This

means going to parties even when you do not feel like it, watching fashion shows, participating in conferences (or even better – lecturing or otherwise contributing content to them), registering for professional seminars, joining professional delegations abroad, joining professional associations, lecturing at the university, publishing professional articles, sometimes even hiring a public relations person.

Most importantly – it is not enough to take these steps. A person invited to a private event, who then sits silently at his table the entire evening, accomplishes nothing. It is important to talk, to be interested, to listen to the other people and interest them. It is vital to know how to present yourself properly and to come prepared, also with accessories. For example, do not come to an event without a business card, or with a card written in a language that says nothing to the participants in the event, or with an embarrassing card that radiates the exact opposite of what you have managed to radiate. If you have managed to radiate a successful image, it would be foolish to offer a business card that reeks of amateurism, negligence and failure.

If you are only going to take one piece of advice out of this chapter, let it be the following: It is important to dedicate time, even much time, consistently and over many years, to making connections with people and to networking. This will require considerable amounts of money for meals and travel, conferences and membership in organizations, clothing and items such as business cards and promotional materials. In the beginning this may seem to you like a waste of time. Instead of spending a quiet evening at home, in front of the TV or out of doors with your wife or husband, you go to a distant place, listen to a boring lecture and have some refreshments (sometimes not so fresh) with a group of people that you do not know, some of them boring or jerks straight from hell. At the end of the evening you have run up a huge bill, you didn't enjoy yourself that much and you not only missed seeing your favorite TV show but also lost several hours of sleep, guaranteeing that tomorrow you will be particularly "on edge."

But finally in the end it will pay off – there is no better way to find a business partner or an investor. There is no better way to locate professionals and to form a sincere opinion about them. In my view, this is even one of the best ways to create goodwill, a good reputation and to gain recognition. The more people know you, the more work and opportunities will flow your way. Maybe, surprisingly and without even thinking about it, you will become somebody else's investor or partner, or be exposed to new and amazing ideas. Whether or not you can admit this, even if you are the Albert Einstein of the present century, still, most of the good ideas in the world (or even in your country) will certainly not come from you.

I can testify, from my own experience, that if I weighed the "cost" of the time I have invested in all of these events, plus the actual costs – for each dollar that I have invested, I have received around 100. And it has not taken many years. Show me another investment channel that will yield more money for you over time (maybe Bill Gates, Warren Buffett or Carlos Slim will disagree with me here – but of course, these are only three people, and I'm sure that they invested – and still invest – in networking, even though certainly less than they did in the past).

Beyond financial expedience, getting together with other like-minded individuals is extraordinarily satisfying – along the road you will easily gain new friends. Human interaction is immensely interesting, and some of these interactions are simply fun. What could be wrong with a good meal, or stealing a glance at a model, who is walking next to you scantily dressed? What could be wrong with listening to reports of the most advanced and fascinating developments in your field of practice? What do you have against listening to good jokes or watching a good show?

And perhaps the greatest satisfaction – what can be wrong with knowing that you made it on your own, thanks to your own brilliant ideas and abilities?

Finally, ask yourself six simple questions:

1. Have I ever used any of the excuses from the beginning of this chapter, or a similar excuse?
2. Do I regularly invest in networking?
3. Am I investing, at least as described in this chapter (both time and money), in expanding my social networks and interacting with other people?
4. If I have a new and amazing idea tomorrow and I look for someone to help me – an investor or a partner – can I phone at least twenty different people right then and there, whom I know, who may be able to help, and who might be interested?
5. Do I know people in the field of public relations, or who are very "networked" and have excellent social skills?
6. Have I ever managed to establish a business venture or a financial success thanks to a social contact?

If you answered "yes" to at least one of these questions, and certainly if several or all of these questions – you certainly have something to learn and to apply from this chapter. This lesson may be one of the most important ones for you to assimilate into your life, especially when it comes to your financial success.

"Culvis dolori remedium est patientia."   *"Patience is the cure for all suffering."*

Publilius Syrus, Sententiae

CHAPTER 10

Patience and Forbearance, Sowing and Reaping

This is probably the shortest chapter in the book.

It is short for a simple reason – it is about one of the worst mistakes on the road to success: impatience. Patience is among the most important qualities of a winner. That old Hebrew maxim - "What may not be achieved by your plans may well be won with time" – exists for a reason.

In the beginning of the book we reviewed the various roads to financial success, and quite surprisingly – the only ways that do not require patience are winning the lottery or being born with a silver spoon in one's mouth. Patience is actually a psychological problem that goes back to childhood. We have a hard time delaying gratification, and when we believe that we deserve something and yet do not get it, we are swamped by hard feelings. When this dissatisfaction continues long enough – these hard feelings intensify and manifest as frustration and depression.

Due to those feelings we often miss opportunities for success, or worse – make rash decisions that end very badly and cannot possibly end well.

Consider this – there are no magic solutions, no free lunches, no magic cures. People only become rich overnight in fairy tales, not in real life. Do you think that you have what it takes to succeed? Keep at it and be patient. If you're doing the right things, time will take care of your success.

Regarding patience – this quality is also necessary when making financial decisions.

Let us take for example, a reasonable person who has a rather modest goal – he wishes to live comfortably for many years, without having to work. If possible, he would also like to afford, for example, a few vacations with his family in luxury hotels around the world every year (as a non-working person…). If he adjusts his lifestyle to this goal, even without achieving phenomenal success he will still accumulate an amount of money that will certainly give him several such years (though not many) at a relatively young age. Regarding patience, in actual fact many of these "winners" simply consume their savings in the pursuit of short-term pleasures (they do not delay their gratification), losing the much greater (several times over!) added value of the future.

Another important point: the reality we live in is fickle and subject to changes. What is not feasible or doable today may well be a possibility in another year or two, or perhaps in five or ten years. In countless cases someone chooses a particular path, despairs of it too quickly and moves on, only to realize in retrospect that had they persevered for several more years, they would have now been in an entirely different place. While the feeling of frustration is indeed unpleasant, the feeling of having missed one's opportunities, when one is forced to regret his past decisions, is a much tougher pill to swallow – as another old Hebrew saying goes, "Think before you act."

Life always presents us with opportunities. I think that it is always better to have missed one because you were being patient, than to have made a critical, careless error. Indecision is of course a very negative quality, but impulsiveness, when one makes un-informed, rash decisions, is quite as destructive. One must find the right balance. A successful, wealthy and rational person must have a method for making quick decisions but never reckless ones. Patience generally pays off, even if it causes some short-term damage or frustration. Religious Jews have a maxim that applies here very well – "any delay is for the better." Beyond being an op-timistic, positive way of thinking, this maxim reflects a universal truth. Generally, when one looks from a perspective of time, every-thing progresses for the better. Shares and bonds may be the best example for this.

THE TOOLBOX FOR CHAPTER TEN – PATIENCE AND FORBEARANCE, SOWING AND REAPING

Always be patient. This holds true in every area of life. Avoid making rash decisions – always be reasonable and prudent. Set for yourself a meaningful, long-term objective, maybe two, and many short-term ones, simpler to achieve. Make patience a keystone of every area in your life, especially in your financial

conduct and regarding the question of how your money "behaves" or is invested.

If you are impatient by nature, try working on this and showing improvement – patience is a critical quality for success. If you have not managed to control your behavior or feelings over the years, then whenever you have a more balanced moment, put yourselves in situations that force you to be patient. Several ways to do this are: a) investing an amount of money in a long-term savings plan, which may only be broken with a heavy fine; b) committing to a real-estate purchase; or – c) signing long-term employment contracts. With such commitments and frameworks, even a very "short-fused" individual can be trained to exhibit patience in his conduct and acts.

"Fortes fortuna adiuvat."   *"Luck favors the bold."*

Cicero, Tusculanae disputationes

CHAPTER 11

Self-discipline and Courage

Wiser people than I have said that luck favors the bold. Cicero is only one of them. I ran into similar adages during my officers training course at Bahad 1 military training base. Our slogan as officers was "only he who dares wins" – in the same spirit of Cicero's words. Perhaps an even more accurate statement is this: "Only he who dares and persists wins."

Every day we meet people with potential, who do not realize it. They are bitter and frustrated, generally blaming their hard luck or harsh fate. A few of them may well have been very unlucky. Statistically, this does happen. Nevertheless, most of them - and I will say it in the rudest way – are cowards, and lead a coward's life. The frustration they feel is the coward's frustration. Their bitterness and unrealized potential is the price that the coward pays for his cowardice in a world that mostly assists the brave.

Who has never met (or never felt this way himself) a person who works at a certain job and thinks that he can do other things, more marvelous and exciting? Who has never met a person who thinks that he can be a better manager than his boss? We see this every day, and still, all of these people mark time, sometimes even for decades. Their feelings of disgust, nausea and frustration only become intensified with every passing day. They expect the change to happen of itself, that someone "up there" will notice their unique talents and offer them the ladder to the top, the opportunity, the promotion, the change they yearn for. But personally they do not do anything that would bring them closer to realizing their wishes – and so nothing ever happens, in most cases…

Think for yourselves for a moment – how many of you (or of your acquaintances) think that you (or they) deserve to earn more than you do now? How many of you think that you deserve a promotion at work, and that you are more capable than other people, whose social or financial standing is higher than yours? How many of you would be glad to make a change in your lives?

Now take another moment and try to answer this: How many of these people, who (for example) are interested in a promotion at work, are actually asking for it very directly? How many of them actively seek other employment? How many of them go to interviews or prepare CVs? How many of them quit their jobs and try their luck in a field that they really like, in a job that interests them?

Most people simply fear changes – including positive changes. Even more people fear risks, and the overwhelming majority submits to the comforts of their present life. We like to chatter, to complain, to envy – but when it comes to taking action, cowardice tends to defeat any other consideration.

An average person has many obligations – a family, children, a mortgage, expenses – and can generally meet all of them. Now, he believes, any change, especially if he has become accustomed to a routine over many years – may collapse the tower he has built.

And so, a person who could have been an entrepreneur, a millionaire with many assets, may well work all his life as an employee and never realize his potential, just because he is more comfortable going on like this for the moment. It is sad to say, but this holds true for most of us. The older we grow, the more fixed we become, the more we fear change and the more we limit our own development.

Self-discipline is another aspect of courage, I feel, which is why I put both qualities together in this chapter. Persisting in what you do, especially if you get long-lasting negative feedback from your environment, is an act of bravery. Setting your own objectives, striving to reach them and persisting in so doing despite all difficulties – this takes courage. Overriding your own qualities that would take you in the opposite direction, delaying gratification and acting against your own nature, for the long term, in order to accomplish objectives – this is courageous conduct. Courage, of course, also implies taking risks.

One of the problems along the road is that the border between courage and foolishness is not very well-defined. In my view, one should take calculated risks, but not every calculated risk is necessarily perceived as such. The following example will illustrate this.

I once participated in a seminar at Tel Aviv University, and one of our guests was Prof. Ian Ayres, who presented an article he had written: "Buying Stock on Margin can Reduce Retirement Risk." I will not go very deeply into this; I will only mention a single amazing detail. The esteemed professor examined data from stock exchanges, shares and bonds from around the world over the last 130 years. He made mathematical calculations and created a fairly stable model, which gave rise to the following conclusion: when a person purchases shares at a young age with money that he does not have, by taking loans and paying interest on them, when he reaches retirement age he will have a much greater amount of money than another person – he will be wealthier.

This model proved its validity also in the presence of stock-exchange crashes, such as the one in 1929, or those that we have experienced ourselves in 2008 and in 2011. Even if an investor enters the stock exchange a day before the crash, he still gains considerable amounts of money in the long term. In actual fact, the level of risk that such a person runs when he takes loans and buys shares with that money (this is mathematically proven) is even lower than that of a person who invests 100% of his money in shares! I want to clarify this – it is scientifically and mathematically proven that even if you obtain credit on the eve of a crash, and buy shares with that money and with every single dollar that you own on Earth – so long as you can pay the installments on the loan in the long run, you will gain more than in any other investment channel.

And so, thanks to a retrospective analysis of the markets since 1870, we see that a type of conduct that we all perceive as dangerous and irresponsible – taking loans to buy shares – proves itself in the long run and is finally much less dangerous and much more profitable than taking a mortgage to buy an apartment, for example.

 ## THE TOOLBOX FOR CHAPTER ELEVEN – SELF-DISCIPLINE AND COURAGE

- A person who does not take risks, is actually taking the greatest risk, which is also 100% likely to come true. In fact, such a person waives his potential to succeed and become wealthy. As I see it, the loss of potential to become wealthy is one of the greatest risks. A person who does not care about this probably has another set of considerations, and financial strength (and this book) will not be his highest concern.

- Persistent self-discipline requires courage. For example, it was proven again and again that in the long term, it pays to stick to one's investments even when the stock exchange crashes.

- Complaints, chattering, frustration and blaming fate or luck are the way a coward behaves.

- Brave people do not talk. They take action.

- An extreme act that appears dangerous is not necessarily so. Oftentimes, in a long-term perspective, it proves to be the less dangerous path. A clear example of this is taking a loan to purchase shares, as described by Prof. Ayres. Quitting one's job is another example. Looking for a job while still being employed is yet another one.

- Always take calculated risks and keep a contingency plan – a Plan B and perhaps even a Plan C. Life is fickle and things will not always happen the way you want them to. Prepare both for failure as well as a rainy day.

And perhaps another point that I did not mention so far: there is no shame in trying and failing. Quite the contrary – the very fact of having tried adds to one's honor, proving that one is courageous and daring. Shameful is the person who has never tried. A person who quits his job and goes out to pursue a dream, starts a business and after a while understands that the business will not propel itself and "comes back with his tail between his legs" to his former job or to a similar one, should, in my view, be highly appreciated.

By the way, most people will get an immediate sense of schaden-freude, when they hear of the failure of the person who has tried, and for the simple reason that it makes them feel more comfortable with their own cowardice. If, for example, a colleague of yours quits his job to start a business, and five years later he becomes a multi-millionaire while you remain in the same place, you will probably feel frustration, envy and perhaps regret for not having done some-thing similar yourselves. In the opposite case, you can tell yourself with satisfaction: he "burned" three years of his life, while I made strides. But is it really so? Did that person "burn" three years? Did you really open a considerable gap over him? Usually this is not the case, and even failure has its value – of course, so long as one keeps trying.

Remember – you must not despair. If you persist, show self-discipline and courage and try again and again, even in the face of fail-ure – one of two things will happen: either you will finally make it big (though perhaps later than you have planned), or you will reach the end of your life without the success that you have wished for, but at least knowing that you have tried to realize your potential.

By the way, if you conduct yourself responsibly and prudently (including savings, insurances and so on), then even in case you "fail" you will not really fail. It may well be that your failure to meet the high objectives that you have set for yourselves will still be well beyond other people's successes, as the success of such people is limited by conservatism and cowardice, or simply because our society has pushed them to a corner, which they could not leave. Western society is exactly rigged for this – to delimit most of us within the middle class, perhaps even the lower middle class; to extract from us everything possible in order to enrich a few people at the top of the pyramid, and to throw us away when we become old as used merchandise, no longer useful.

If you do not act as expected, you may also change the predicted outcome. In order to do this, as we said above, the qualities required are courage, self-discipline and of course patience.

CHAPTER 12

Savings, Pension and Contingency Plans for Failures

Most of us tend to see the future through rose-colored glasses, especially after reading a book such as this one. It is difficult for us to think that the future may hold failure for us, disappointment or both. I'm sure that quite a few of you will nod to yourselves after finishing this book, telling yourselves under your breath that your future is guaranteed.

It is important to remember though – nothing in life is certain. Even if you are bright, lucky, talented, persistent and equipped with the suitable qualities for enrichment and financial success – it is not sure that you will accomplish that. There are too many variables in the "database" of your life, many of which are completely random or almost so.

The Israel Defense Forces use the concept of a "contingency

plan." The contingency plan (literally "drawer plan"), is one that should not come into being if everything goes right – it is only there in the case of an extreme, unusual or unexpected outcome. Actually, the very existence of this plan tells us that despite the low likelihood of its occurrence and the basic premise that it should not occur, a plan was prepared to help us face the possibility of a strange/unusual scenario, as part of a risk-management policy.

This is exactly what we have to do in our personal lives. We need to lay down a basic premise based on success, but also prepare a strong alternative plan in the event of failure - even though in my view, one can turn any failure into success; at least into relative success, in any case.

It is important to remember – excessive conservatism and prudence will necessarily reduce the chances of success. Conversely, lack of caring may lead to another type of extreme situation. One must adopt an approach that contains a certain measure of conservatism, while still leaving considerable leeway, guaranteeing that at least towards the end of your life, once you retire on a pension, you will be "slightly wealthy." A slightly wealthy person is indeed worse off than a vastly wealthy one, but is still much better off than a slightly poor or a vastly poor person.

It is important that you be aware of the possibility of failure already at a young age, and prepare for that ahead of time. Timely preparation guarantees success in facing this hurdle, thanks to the interest that may be compounded through a long-term saving plans.

To illustrate this, let us assume that an average saver earns a 1% real interest rate per year on his savings, and that his retirement age is 65. If a 20-year-old person sets aside $1,000 from his salary for a pension plan, when he reaches the age of retirement, this amount will have developed into exactly NIS 5,841. Conversely, if he sets aside the $1,000 at age 45, the amount will only become NIS 2,191.

Notice the effect of compound interest! Assume that this person, in order to maintain his current standard of living, will need $6,000 regularly every month once he reaches age 65, and that he will live until age 80, or 15 years after retiring.

As amazing as this may sound, in order to guarantee a stable, handsome income of $6,000 every month (maybe a little more) after retirement, all the saver will have to do is set aside $1,000 every month – if, of course, he does so at the right moment – at age 20. If he starts setting aside the same amounts at age 45 – his regular monthly income will only be about $2,000 once he reaches retirement. Exactly one-third. I want to stress, as I mentioned earlier, that in a long-term view (data spanning the period 1870 – 2016), it was found that changing market conditions, momentary crises and even harsh worldwide financial crises do not really matter, and that even the plans that are considered riskier in the long term balance out and guarantee (at least) an average, reasonable return on investment throughout the period – so long as one can still keep setting aside the relevant amounts over the long term.

In day-to-day life, a provision of $1,000 every month is quite affordable. This amount will not endanger your long-term plans and will not significantly affect your roadmap to success and to enrichment. Most of us spend larger amounts every month on things we don't need – on unattractive clothing, a gourmet meal in a restaurant, an unnecessary trip and other expenses that one can easily cut down on.

And what is the meaning of this slight "tightening of the belt" that we undertake? Let us take another look at our guy, the 20-year-old, who sets aside $1,000 every month for a pension plan and does so for 45 years until he reaches age 65. How much money will he accumulate? Well, enough to create ongoing revenues of about $12,000 each month until the end of his life – for fifteen years. Had our guy set aside $2,000 every month, he would enjoy a steady monthly income of $24,000 until the end of his life, and so on.

For most of us, such a provision at age 20 is significant, but not impossible. The older we become, this provision really becomes negligible for us. For many of us, the workplace will set aside much bigger amounts for our pension.

As this book is being written, a monthly income of NIS 12,000 (or about $3,500) is quite normal in Israel, affording one a reasonable standard of living.

THE TOOLBOX FOR CHAPTER TWELVE – SAVINGS, PENSION AND CONTINGENCY PLANS FOR FAILURES

My message here is clear: make savings (especially pension plans) a high priority. Do not neglect to save money. Start at the earliest possible age. Take risks elsewhere. Reserve the same amount for your savings every month –$1,000, or 1,500, 2,000, 2,500 and so on, according to your capabilities. Treat this amount as if you have never earned it. It will be an additional insurance policy of sorts – insurance for quality of life, or a policy against failure.

If you do become wealthy, this amount will be negligent for you and you will not be sorry for having saved it. You will also not need it when you grow old. But if you did not manage to become wealthy, this amount will be your consolation, your success and your support when you become old. It will not turn you into a man of great wealth – but you will not be poor. The tiny amount that you have set aside every month can easily place you in the higher band of the middle class in your country – you might even scratch the wealthy class from below.

I believe that every person is born with an immense financial potential. Many people never consummate their potential, and when they leave the world the leave behind them very few material assets, sometimes even debts. If you save, you guarantee that you realize at least a part of your financial potential. More than that – you will get to enjoy it.

One last point to conclude this chapter of the book: It is important not to save too much. A too-large amount set aside from your account every month will weigh heavily on your growth potential, on your ability to take risks and to invest, and perhaps worst of all – it will also interfere with your enjoyment of life itself. If you cannot do significant things in your life because of savings – save less. It is very sad to see a person save and save, denying himself and his family basic needs, and then die prematurely without enjoying the fruits of his labor in the slightest – and many people are like that. Don't end up in that category.

CHAPTER 13

The Cost of Useless Emotions

This chapter has a single purpose – to clarify that some of the emotions and qualities so praised by society, those that society urges us to adopt since childhood, are actually useless, limiting and overbearing, and are meant to squash an individual and his inherent potential. Those qualities and sentiments (some of which are imposed by society) are used by others to crush your lives and dominate them, to intimidate you and to push you into situations that you will not be able to come out of. If you become aware of these emotions and shake them off, you will be on the good road to success.

I will start with the most despicable feeling, in my view – shame. I quote the Wikipedia definition of "shame," as of the day I am writing this chapter (I highlighted a few bits that bear upon the point I wish to stress):

"Shame is a negative feeling. It involves **inconvenience around people**. Shame is related to certain thought patterns and to typical physiological reactions – such as blushing and stammering. A prototype of the feeling of shame is the story of Adam and Eve, who hid from God among the trees of the garden, after eating from the tree of knowledge (Book of Genesis 3:8). The concept underlying shame robs a person of his humanity and of his being born in God's image, equal to all men. **A person sees himself as being inferior to others, sometimes as being bereft of any value or importance**. The great problem with shame is that it **prevents a person from fully functioning in the world and realizing himself. It sticks a person in his current situation and does not allow him to make progress**. Even if he does, **it is difficult for him to realize his inherent potential**. It may cause certain people to withdraw and isolate themselves, or to wear a mask when they are in company.

"Its advantage is that it prevents some of the anti-social activities and crimes that harm society – the individual will refrain from doing them because of his fear of being caught and feeling shame. According to Jean-Paul Sartre, shame is the inconvenience created when one becomes an object. To illustrate this, Sartre brings the example of a person who peeks through a keyhole at the people inside the room. In this situation, that person is the subject and the people he watches are objects to him. Once another person arrives and catches the peeper – he immediately becomes an object and begins to feel shame. According to Sartre, the humanity robbed from the person who feels shame, is his independence at being the observer, not the object for observation.

"According to another definition of the exact nature of the humanity robbed from the person who feels shame – 'humanity' is the ability to hide. Shame is caused because a person's confidence in being able to hide things – bad or otherwise – from other people, is shaken. Shame is among the toughest feelings for people, alongside pain and fear. Sometimes people (especially from the high classes) prefer to commit suicide when caught at various offenses, rather than face this feeling – this was very common in Japanese culture. Due to its intensity, this emotion is used in public punishment, in order to deter potential offenders.

"In antiquity and in the middle ages, shame was part and parcel of the punishment methods used. The pillory or the stocks were typical examples of this. According to Chazal (the wise Jewish thinkers of the past), a part of the punishment of sinners, such as a deviant wife or other people who were sentenced to flogging, was shaming them. In some places, defendants or suspects were made to go out with a wooden board attached to their back, with a writing that disgraced them. **This sanction, of humiliation and shaming, was more powerful than a monetary or a physical punishment.** Punishment by shaming is still prevalent in various places in the world. For example: a person who dirties the street in Singapore is punished by having to clean the street himself while wearing eye-catching clothes. His picture is then published in the papers."

OK – this is quite enough. The Wikipedia entry is much longer and goes on and on (and on). I have only brought a summary of the essence of this entry. As you know, Wikipedia entries are changed and edited every day – they keep developing over time. Nevertheless, I am sure that even at this stage of the chapter you already understand me well and can predict my next words: **If you are not criminals, shame has no place in your lives. I will go as far as saying that even some offenses, as they are defined by our society,**

do not carry shame and that even the law does not attribute "moral turpitude" to those who perpetrate them.

Should a person be ashamed because he wants more material assets?

Should he be ashamed of having tried to start a business and failed?

Should anybody be ashamed because he is driving an older car than his friends, or because his home is smaller or poorer than theirs?

In my view, shame is a completely unnecessary emotion. It is utterly useless for a strong, capable person. Who are these "others" that we should be ashamed in front of? What is this feeling, that is going to make us limit ourselves and not do things that would help us to progress?

Many people are ashamed to ask for a raise. They know that if their salary rises, they will receive more money than their colleagues. The organization is willing to grant the raise if they ask for it – but because of shame, or for fear of hearing "no," the employee does not ask for the raise. Another example: take a military or an academic organization – a young soldier or student is afraid to ask the commander or the professor a question, fearing the shame they may experience if the question seems stupid – especially if a large audience is present. This is first-class nonsense! Ultimately, the student will take the exam without knowing all of the material and the soldier will risk his life because he failed to understand an important detail. And why? Because they fear the reactions of others? Who are these "others," other than people like you, or maybe even your inferiors!

Maybe in twenty more years, our student will be a much more

senior professor than the one he is afraid to ask? Maybe in twenty more years our soldier will become a general?

It is very likely that a person controlled by shame will remain that soldier or that student throughout his life and will never become a general or a professor. A person who feels shame in front of other people probably feels, deep in his heart, that he is inferior to them. If he obeys this feeling and acts upon it, his achievements will really be inferior to theirs.

I can name many people (I'm sure that you can also) who lack skills and insight. They may be complete dunces, but as they have high self-confidence, and most importantly – have no shame, they today occupy very senior positions and functions.

Against these, I can name (and again, I'm sure that you can name many more) talented, wise and worthy people who are stuck in all sorts of inferior jobs, and their bosses are those same people who lack skills and brains. This is only because throughout their lives, these talented people have let feelings of fear, shame and humility dictate their behavior.

In some cases, a person had better feel shame – when he deviates from his own standards and from the collective ones. Usually these are cases of severe criminal offenses that also carry shame and condemnation. Shame is proper in such cases. **But these are the extreme cases. They are completely unrelated to the shame that most people feel**.

We have discussed humility at some length in this book, especially in chapter 8 ("Reporting to Seniors; Reports from Subordinates"). This can be best summarized by the maxim. **"You did but failed to tell about it – so you didn't do!"**

In certain situations, a bit of humility goes a long way – but such situations are rare. It is important not to cross the border into arrogant behavior, but bear firmly in mind that **most people over-inflate their deeds and tend to adorn themselves with borrowed plumes. If you minimize your acts in the name of humility, this might be a serious error that would position you far behind.** Take two men for example, both attorneys. One achieves a favorable result in about 50% of his cases, but on social occasions and when meeting potential clients, he only talks about his successes. He never mentions his failures or any embarrassing details. When recounting his successes, he spices them with colorful additions and exaggerations. People who talk with him certainly consider that he is exaggerating, as most people do, and as they hear from him 100% success stories, that are great enough to sound like 120%, they suppose that his success rate is 80%.

The other attorney is much more capable. He helps his clients win about 80% of their cases, but unlike the first attorney, due to his integrity (yes, I know, an attorney with integrity, some of you will make fun of this idea…) and humble nature, he never neglects to mention his failures (they are not so bad! Only 20%!) and does not over-emphasize his successes – he just tells them as they are. What will his interlocutors conclude? That of course, he exaggerates as much as everybody else. If he claims 80% success, he probably wins only 50% of his cases, maybe less.

Look at the results: The attorney who does well 50% of the time is publicly seen as one who wins 80%, while the attorney who does win 80% of his cases, and should be seen as his mirror image, is seen as only winning 50% of his cases.

The difference stems from humility – and the damage is huge. It is quite possible that the less successful attorney will earn more, dare to charge higher hourly fees (as he has no shame or humility) and so attract more clients. The absurdity of it is that it is exactly his higher prices that will seem to prove his professional skills, in the eyes of many, thereby further widening the gap between himself and his humble colleague. **In public, it is exactly those people who are seen as "shameless" and recover from failures, who do better. Take Donald Trump as an example.** It is important to stress that I am totally against fraud and misrepresentation – but I think that doing and not telling, being overly humble, is a deadly sin. It is important to do and important to tell the tale.

The last quality that I will mention here is hesitancy. Hesitancy is a manifestation of fear. You come by a good opportunity and you convince yourself that there are many reasons – which may well be nonexistent in actuality, maybe these are only possible scenarios – to refrain from seizing it. We are familiar with such stories, and not only in the realm of business. How many men hesitated to ask a maiden's hand in marriage, only to miss the love of their life and the mother of their children. Others hesitated to study the profession they loved, choosing instead a boring profession that seemed to offer better financial prospects. Some people hesitated and failed to buy the apartment they desired, and later the prices rose and they could never afford their dream apartment after that.

Hesitancy is a roadblock to success. The opportunistic winner knows how to recognize opportunities and seize them.

THE TOOLBOX FOR CHAPTER THIRTEEN – THE COST OF USELESS EMOTIONS

Try to get rid of sensations and feelings that might slow you down and wreck your potential for success.

If you are not murderers, rapists, thieves or perverts (beyond acceptable limits…) – do not allow shame into your lives.

Usually humility does not contribute to success. It is only proper once you have already made it, or in forums, in which you are clearly the best or the most senior player, the one everybody envies. If a social gap already exists in your favor, it's OK to act humble.

Hesitancy is a stumbling block. When opportunities present themselves – seize them. Nevertheless, don't cast prudence and care aside – it is important not to cross the border into rash behavior. Look for a good balance.

This is important: Remember that you are not less worthy – perhaps even worthier than others. You deserve more than you have today. If you believe this, not only will this eventually happen, you will also get rid of such negative qualities as shame along the way.

Perhaps most importantly – there is no shame in failure. Quite the contrary – it is much more disgraceful to never try at all. Whoever claims otherwise is perhaps trying to make you fail. If you are sure that this person is well-intentioned, then he is not gifted with the necessary qualities for success, quite unfortunately. It is very likely that the person who tries to make you feel ashamed of having tried and failed, is not a successful person in his field.

CHAPTER 14

Wastefulness, Gambling and Stupidity

Wastefulness, gambling and stupidity are synonymous in many senses. We have already spoken about the value of the money you have in your youth. A dollar saved at age 20 is not equivalent to a dollar saved at age 80. Assuming that a man lives to 80 on average, one dollar in the 80-year-old's account is worth exactly one dollar, as far as he's concerned. That same dollar, saved by the 20-year-old, will be worth approximately nine dollars by the time he turns 80, due to that invisible value that money accumulates over time. A dollar saved at an early age will yield many dollars without any risk, the older one grows.

Therefore, wastefulness at a young age has much heavier implications than wastefulness when one grows old. The result is similar with gambling – actually even worse. Take a lottery ticket, for example. Let us say that the chances to win the first prize are one in ten million, a ticket costs $10 and the first prize is $2 million. Assuming no sub-prizes, the expected value of any lottery ticket is only twenty cents, but you will pay ten dollars for it! Let us say that with the sub-prizes, the ticket is worth two dollars. In this case, the immediate loss upon its purchase is equal to eight dollars on average.

An 80-year-old man who buys a ticket loses eight dollars at that very moment.

But what about the 20-year-old man? He loses seventy-two dollars and even more!

Let us say that you purchase a lottery ticket every week, from age 20 until age 80. There are 52 weeks in a year. In the first year alone, you will actually lose 3,744 dollars without even noticing. You will only spend 35 dollars a month – but this is the actual loss obtained! Had you saved the same amount in a solid retirement plan, that would be the amount obtained!!

I will explain why this is stupid. Say that you are a gambler by nature. You care about the win, not about the financial loss along the way. If you wait and delay your gratification, you will be able to participate in 468 lottery drawings for the same amount that you had paid for 52. You increase your chances ninefold for the same amount of money!

If we could choose between paying a certain amount to win money, or paying one-ninth of that amount, buying whatever we want with the remainder and still having chances to win the jackpot – most of us would pick the second option.

 ## THE TOOLBOX FOR CHAPTER FOURTEEN – WASTEFULNESS, GAMBLING AND STUPIDITY

Old people can afford heavier bets. Old people are entitled to waste their money. Obviously, they would still have to do this within certain limits, but a young man who takes the same risks as those taken by the elder, is actually risking nine times as much!

And how many of us know risk-loving old people? Of those people we know, most of those who take financial risks are young.

Remember this rule of thumb: wastefulness = stupidity; gambling = stupidity. The younger you are, the more stupid you are if you behave like that!

Those who live off of this human weakness are the casinos, "Mifal HaPayis" in Israel and in general – any enterprise that relies upon drawings. It is OK to participate from time to time for a small amount – but nothing more, and if one must develop this bad habit, it's better to do it at the latest possible age.

CHAPTER 15

The Importance of General Knowledge and Conversational Skills

Conversational skills are among the most important abilities for anyone who wishes to succeed, simply because other people do not spend whole days with you, but only brief moments in life. Even those people we tag as "very familiar to us" we do not know that well. We know a certain aspect that they exhibit outwards, for a limited period of time, and we may only spend several minutes truly interacting with them every time we meet them, in the best of cases.

People who recognize this fact are not shocked when they hear stories about women who discover that their husbands were having an affair behind their backs for years, or neighbors who discover that their beloved cat-loving neighbor is actually a vicious serial killer and a cannibal. We cannot really know a person based on the interaction (which generally amounts to light conversation) we have with them in daily life. Sometimes we cannot even know the person who lives with us permanently, our spouse. And what about most of our human interactions?

Very simply – most of those around you do not know you deeply, and the older you become, the number of people who really know you becomes smaller and smaller. Most people form an opinion about you and your personality on the basis of a first impression or a secondary impression only. Your conversational skills are a significant factor in creating these impressions.

I will return to the well-known Cicero quote in the beginning of this chapter. It expresses a simple idea – it is not necessary to talk much in order to create a positive impression. If you speak wisely and to the point, even a few inarticulate words or a stutter will generally bring better results than senseless verbosity. It is better to refrain from talking at all than to talk nonsense and be seen as a blabbermouth. We all know that "silence is golden" – if you are an idiot, so long as you do not open your mouth, your stupidity remains unexposed.

The facts are simple – most people have a two-way interaction with you for a very limited time during the day. One-way interaction (for example, a lecture or a speech) is also relatively limited in time, but the communication and the situation are almost entirely under your control.

So far, we have three very obvious main conclusions:

One – most people do not really know you and mostly rely on a first or a secondary impression;

Two – you have limited interaction with most people;

Three – It is not necessarily a good thing to talk much. In certain situations, it is better to remain silent or to say little.

Interestingly enough, in modern society people tend to over-specialize. Nowadays, human knowledge is so extensive and expansive, that even the greatest scholars must focus on a very narrow field of knowledge.

Take medicine for example. Just 400 years ago, an intelligent person could carry around in his brain a considerable part of the medical knowledge that existed in the world and be a prodigious doctor. He could even be prodigious in several fields at the same time (Leonardo Da Vinci immediately comes to mind as a striking example). Is this possible nowadays? Of course not. Nowadays, an intelligent doctor who was the best student in high school and in university may invest all of his efforts on a single disease and on a single procedure that concerns the middle ear.

As the fields of knowledge are so expansive, in order to be proficient in any field, a smart, brilliant person needs to dedicate many years of his life just to assimilate the foundations of knowledge that concern the narrow niche he deals with.

Due to this specialization in narrow disciplines, many people lack broad general knowledge. They are focused on one area, they are interested in that area and read books about it, dedicating to it most of their time and energy. If they are especially interesting people – they may engage in two fields, perhaps three.

But we are very different from one another. Take the doctor from the above example – how many people are really interested in the middle ear? Perhaps colleagues or the chronically ill. Most of the people the doctor meets in day-to-day life (assuming that he does venture out of the hospital from time to time) are only capable of holding a light, shallow conversation with the doctor and do not impress him greatly.

On the other hand, another person, who knows the basics about the middle ear, will be able to hold a riveting conversation with the doctor and impress him greatly as an intelligent, interesting person. That person will not have to invest ten of his years studying medicine – he may invest less than a day. His level of understanding in this field will be much inferior to the doctor's, who dedicates his life to it, but as his personal interaction with the doctor will be very brief, that time period will allow him to hold a significant, interesting conversation with the doctor and to leave the desired impression upon him. Of course, in a deep conversation, the professional will understand that his interlocutor has limited knowledge in the field (he never claimed otherwise), but this is not the "usual" situation, and even in such an extreme case, the professional will probably still consider that his interlocutor knows much more than the usual layman and form a good, effective first impression about him.

In order to develop a casual conversation on many subjects, it is important to acquire general knowledge – lots of it. A broad general knowledge guarantees that in any audience you find yourself in – you can always present yourself as an interesting, attractive and smart conversationalist. General knowledge also increases your opportunities over time. If earlier you could only hold a meaning-ful conversation with a small percentage of those you met, after you accumulate a wider knowledge base, you significantly increase the number of people, with whom you can hold a meaningful conversation.

As unbelievable as this may sound (sorry for this cynical com-ment) – it is important to understand that you and your field of interest are not the center of the world. Our graveyards are full of "indispensable people." It is quite possible that your occupation or hobby intrigues you and that you dedicate all of your spare time to it, but for most people it is boring to death, a total waste of time. This does not mean that one of you is right and the other is wrong. There are so many fields of human knowledge and people differ so greatly, that it is only natural to have great gaps in the levels of interest associated with a particular subject. For use in low-level interactions, there is no reason not to acquire basic knowledge also in the less-familiar fields that interest you less.

Last but not least – beyond improving your conversational skills, the impression you leave and the new opportunities that become available to you, general knowledge will significantly contribute to you in yet another way: it may lead you to new ideas, associations and skills that you wouldn't reach without it.

THE TOOLBOX FOR CHAPTER FIFTEEN – THE IMPORTANCE OF GENERAL KNOWLEDGE AND CONVERSATIONAL SKILLS

Do not limit yourself to a single field. Beware of that. Dedicate significant amounts of time to acquiring general knowledge in fields that are quite remote from your occupation or main hobby, preferably fields that interest you or pose an intellectual challenge.

Do not be afraid to use your general knowledge and to showcase it at every opportunity, but remember the maxim from the beginning of this chapter – it is sometimes better to say little and listen a lot.

Most of the interpersonal interactions you will have in life will not be intensive – they will be short-term. This datum can work in your favor you many ways, so long as you have broad general

knowledge.

Most importantly – once you reach a certain standard as a professional, it becomes harder and harder to acquire more knowledge. On the other hand, one can acquire general knowledge by investing little. Always think about the "knowledge expectancy" - after a certain stage, when you are already established in your field, you may well benefit more by investing most of your efforts out of your main field of knowledge – i.e., acquiring general knowledge.

"Ibi potest valere populus ubi leges valent.» "Where laws prevail, there can the people prevail."

Publilius Syrus, Sententiae

CHAPTER 16

The Law and Accounting as Friends and as Stumbling Blocks on the Road to Wealth

As I already mention, if I'm not mistaken, apart from being a high-tech person and a businessman, I also have a lawyer's education and I preside over a law firm. In actual fact, my main occupation has been in the field of law in recent years – in particular private international law. I will therefore start this chapter with a short discussion of legal systems and their importance to you. Do not worry, I have no intention to turn this nice book into a boring dissertation on laws and various precedents, or to start a discussion about the legal aspects of different countries, tell interesting legal stories or even engage in legal-philosophical ruminations.

I will be short and practical, similarly to the rest of this book. After a short survey of the law, in which I will explain how it will help you become wealthy, I will lightly touch upon accounting. Of course, I will also try to present the negative aspects of the law on the road to wealth…

By the nature of things, we all live within a particular legal system. In our world, societies do not exist in a state of anarchy. Mainly, the law regulates the behavior of individuals, and generally (in liberal-democratic societies) it allows a considerable amount of freedom to each person, to engage in his own pursuits. The law does limit behavior that is seen as negative by society. It is patently clear that the law constitutes a great barrier to enrichment. For example, it will not allow you to rob another person, or to build upon free land that you do not own. It will ensure that you pay taxes, charges and high customs duties, which you would have otherwise saved. Of course, this also works in the opposite direction – the law guarantees that another person may not rob you or build upon your land, and taxes collected from the toil of others will also serve to construct a public project that will benefit you and not those other people.

Illegal acts can potentially generate lots of money, we all know that. If we glance at the popular Hollywood films, we will discover that there is plenty of money in prostitution, robberies, illegal gambling and extortion, and that even greater amounts of money change hands in the narcotics trade. Of course, I am not planning to tempt you onto that road to wealth. **Quite the contrary – I will tell you how abiding to the law will turn it (the law) into your friend on the road to wealth. If you wish to be wealthy, you must exercise rigor in matters of the law, and watch every step, big or small, throughout the way. This is the only way to make it (big!)** Compliance with the law will help you sleep well at night, and will summon very strong forces to your side (the state, the police, the courts), without any special effort or sacrifice on your part. Perhaps most importantly – I will teach you how you can become wealthy and still live with a clear conscience, without fear of the law.

My first advice – and this also touches upon another chapter in this book – hire first-class professionals (attorneys, lawyers). Do not save on this. If you are preparing a contract to purchase an apartment, or are starting a new company and must consider every aspect of its activities including taxation, and long-term factors, and even if you write your will - working with good professionals will save you a lot of money in the long run, and you will also enjoy the coverage of their professional liability insurance, in case they fail or act negligently. You will find that in many cases, the premium paid to eliminate the risk is very cheap, compared to the actual risk.

The second advice – never knowingly break the law. Always strive to adhere to the letter of the law. This does not mean that you have to be "righteous." Our laws were not written with the expectation that you become "mother Teresa" or anything close to this. The law is written for the average person, the reasonable person. For example, a robbery of $15,000 is considered a serious criminal offense, that may well send a person to prison. On the other hand, when the bank raises the commission charged for each line in bank statements, for example, it earns many millions of dollars without any possible resistance from the clients - a totally legal move that involves no sanction or punishment. A man who betrays his wife (a patently immoral act, in most people's opinion) will not be indicted in any criminal court. There is no law against cheating on your wife (there may be personal sanctions or financial ramifications, such as divorce), but if you do something a lot less severe than cheating on your wife – say, you park your car without a parking permit – you will immediately be convicted in a crime (most of us do not know it or are not aware of this, but yes – illegal parking is a criminal offense; not collecting dog excrement from the pavement is defined as a criminal offense, and more such "pearls" from the legislator's workshop) and fined. The state is actually telling you indirectly: you illegally parked your car? You're an offender! Bear your punishment! You cheated on your wife? You betrayed the trust of the closest person to you? That's not a problem. A great gap exists between what is moral, correct, reasonable and what is not defined as such by law. Sometimes immoral activity is perfectly legal and socially acceptable, and a trivial act that most of us will perform without even thinking, may be defined as problematic or carry a sanction.

My third advice derives from the two previous ones. In borderline cases, avoid breaking the law and contact first-class professionals, to gain their approval.

What do I mean?

In some cases, you must make a decision that falls within the "grey area." In business, this usually involves tax planning issues. I don't wish to bore you and will only mention that in this area, there are three main categories of taxpayer behavior: standard behavior, when one pays the full amount of tax; tax avoidance – which is actually legitimate tax planning – the taxpayer plans his moves in a totally legal manner, and finally pays less tax; and tax evasion – a severe criminal offense where a person avoids taxes, or employs illegitimate, criminal tax planning.

Sometimes, a very thin line separates the legitimate from the criminal, a line that is a matter of legal interpretation. The situation might change from one day to the next, so what is acceptable today becomes criminal and forbidden tomorrow – or vice versa, that which is prohibited today becomes "kosher" tomorrow. Whenever there is a doubt – ask a professional. Obtain a written opinion that confirms that what you are doing is standard, normative and legal – that you complied with the guidelines, and that even a legal expert confirmed this to you, and you paid him in full for a written opinion on the subject. After all this, there is no danger. You will not be charged with criminal liability. Think about it as an insurance policy of sorts – not a very expensive one.

Fourth advice – if the difference between tax planning and simply paying is not significant, it is better to take the high road. You are supposed to pay a tax that amounts to 25% of your profits, but you can reduce that to 21% if you employ complex planning. It is better to pay 25%. Remember the other side of the coin: in case A you are left with 75% of your profits and in case B – 79%. A minor difference. If the absolute amounts are large and the gap really "hurts" (at least psychologically) – you can almost always change the price and make the other party bear the difference – you will pay the higher tax rate, but will also increase your revenues, thereby in actuality "rolling" the tax over to the paying party. It is always better to take the "high road" and one should not take unnecessary risks – especially if one can simply change the pricing and overburden the client, or the other party, with the extra tax, so that you do not have to feel it. In any case, the system in most civilized countries is built in such a way, that taxation leads to a gradual "crawl" upwards in the value of transactions and assets. It is not worth the risk to the integrity of your lives and to your reputation. Most of us are not prepared for long trials with wide publicity, and they generally carry lesser benefits, compared to the potential damage. Beyond this, somebody has to pay for public services and for defense spending, and you are fortunate if you can contribute to all of the wonders required by our society.

A fifth and last advice, to conclude this part of the chapter – the law is made for the ordinary, standard, frequent cases, those that most of us face. It is limited to the legislator's abilities, and by many political and economic constraints. Moreover, also legal interpretation is limited to the cases brought before the courts. Something very interesting happens as a result: many of the non-standard cases have no legal response. Many of the new, dynamic occurrences that life brings, happen much faster than the law or the regulations can advance.

Therefore, it is worth your while to dedicate much time (in the beginning, even a considerable percentage of your time!) to understanding the legal mechanisms that exist in your field. Once you understand them, think about scenarios that are not covered by existing law. This line of thinking will not only lead you to new ideas and ventures, but also to some that will certainly work in the practical world – nobody thought about them before, and they carry a potential for handsome profits. As this is pioneer territory, much time will pass before such ideas become regulated by laws, and significant barriers will be created for new players, who will wish to enter the field. You may assume that at that stage, you will be among the main players in the new field, and its legal regulations will become your interest.

Last but not least – CPAs. Hire their help already at the first stage. You will not believe how much you can profit from this field, that seems strange and boring to most people. You will not believe how much financial benefit you can derive from the knowledge, skills and experience of those who practice in this field. CPAs are not only for rich people. They will help each and every one of us who is not an employee. Those who will employ their services the right way may well become rich. This is an egg-and-chicken situation. Most importantly – even here, similarly to legal regulation, always comply with all of the formal, regulatory requirements that concern you. Always meet at least the standard set in law. It is better to be much above it.

Remember – it is always better to approach any situation with clean hands, moral superiority and the law on your side. You can succeed this way. It may even be more difficult (and certainly more dangerous) to succeed when you cross the lines.

THE TOOLBOX FOR CHAPTER SIXTEEN – THE LAW AND ACCOUNTING AS FRIENDS AND AS STUMBLING BLOCKS ON THE ROAD TO WEALTH

- Never knowingly break the law.
- When there is a doubt, there is no question. Always request and pay for an official, professional opinion, in writing.
- Employ accounting experts, even when your business is "small."
- Find the "blind spot" in legislation in your field. These loopholes in the law and its interpretation are an opportunity to find new ideas and create new business and lots of money.

- If you have become a significant player in the market, avail yourself of the law to create legal barriers for new players. Prevent competition by legitimate means.
- Do not be greedy. If the difference between taking the high road and saving by using tax loopholes is small – pay the tax and avoid the risk. See it as your contribution to society. It is only advisable to increase the risk if the gap is large – and as mentioned above, you can increase profits without increasing risks, if you employ professional services.

—————————————～·—————————————

CHAPTER 17

Saving on Professional Work is the High Road to Poverty

This is a very short chapter, and hopefully "short and to the point." It presents a conclusion that was always self-evident to me, but I learned that many people do not share this notion with me, so I decided to put it in writing.

Some of us live out the maxim: "buys cheaply, pays dearly," or "penny wise and pound foolish." What do I mean? Many of us are tempted to save in the short term, and ultimately suffer huge losses in the long term. This applies especially when one hires a professional – an attorney or a CPA, a doctor or an investment adviser, etc. Here are a few practical illustrative examples:

1. You buy an apartment and save 0.5% of its price by contacting the cheapest lawyer, only to discover that he

neglected his work and the entire investment goes down the drain.

2. You managed to save $1,500 every year on your payments to your CPA, until your books and records were disqualified by the tax authorities, and now you have to pay a tax supplement amounting to $30,000.

3. A person suspected of a certain offense saves $6,000 on legal fees by picking a young, inexperienced lawyer. He finally spends four extra years in prison.

4. You found the cheapest dentist and managed to save $30 on a tooth filling, but you received low-grade, negligent treatment and the dentist used cheap materials. Several years later you have to pay $1,800 for a dental implant, after losing that tooth.

5. An entrepreneur owns 80% of his venture and refuses to give percentage points to outstanding employees and marketing personnel. Ten years later, his company reaches a value of $10 million. Had he given up absolute ownership and contented himself with 50% of the venture, the profits would have reached $100 million – so he now has $8 million instead of $50 million. It is better to hold a low percentage of something valuable, thereby permitting it to develop, than to be the exclusive, or the almost-exclusive owner of a limited enterprise.

THE TOOLBOX FOR CHAPTER SEVENTEEN – SAVING ON PROFESSIONAL WORK IS THE HIGH ROAD TO POVERTY

The lesson I learned from my own experience is unequivocal: Under no circumstances should we save on professionals and compromise on their quality. Savings on professional work almost always lead to financial losses. A short-term saving on costs means high costs in the long run. If you see yourselves as long-distance runners – saving practices are the wrong move, especially when the result matters.

Remember – one has to pay for good, high-quality service. Be fair with your service providers and keep them happy and loyal. Your accountant knows a lot about you and your business, and so does your lawyer. Most of our important service providers hold positions of trust in our lives in one way or another. Even when some of them are not responsible for the most important areas of our lives, they are often responsible for "life itself," as far as we are concerned – even if we tend to treat this lightly.

Therefore, disaster may result from trying to save a hundred bucks on your gas technician or electrician. The same goes for the construction engineer. Misers pay for their vice. You will not only pay much more at the end of the process, you will also suffer greatly along the way.

A personal example in data security: A client chose not to use the services of our company, which he saw as expensive, instead availing himself of an "expert" who charged an attractive price, which matched his standard of expertise... the price differential was about $20 per hour of work (about $400 per month within the expected scope of work). Several months later, the thrifty client's systems were broken into and very sensitive information was stolen, including the credit card numbers of more than 50,000 clients. It goes without saying that the actual damage, including to his reputation, exceeded his savings scores of times over.

This rule also holds true for almost any other field. How do you price an extra year in prison, or the loss of a tooth and the suffering involved in treatments, beyond the financial cost of the dental implant? Beyond the financial damage, how will you price the collapse of your home?

To recapitulate, when it comes to professionals, don't save if you don't have to. The price does not tell the entire story, of course. A high price, or a brand name, does not necessarily mean quality. But if you are clearly convinced that candidate A provides much higher quality than candidate B and the only reason that keeps you from opting for the better service is the price differential – always try to think about the long term, about the catastrophic consequences that might arise, and about what you will think then, in retrospect.

And yet, under certain circumstances (usually involving un-professional manpower), it is precisely the short-time saving that should be preferred – the test of the "catastrophic result" can be a valid indicator when selecting a professional. If you are willing to bear the worst result, and you consider that the expected damage justifies the risk – then very well – save for the short-term and avoid the unnecessary expense.

CHAPTER 18

Mortgages and Wealth, and a Little More on Self-discipline

In this chapter I will mainly discuss mortgages, because a mortgage is the best-understood example of a loan taken to purchase an asset and generate ongoing income (or avoid ongoing expenses). Another reason for choosing exactly the mortgage, rather than other types of loans and monetary commitments, is that so many people are willing to take on this type of debt, but would avoid other types of loans (not necessarily more dangerous), simply due to social conventions and assumptions that are sometimes wrong.

What actually is a mortgage? If you wish to purchase house or apartment X that suits your standard of living and you have some savings, but not enough to purchase the house – your situation is similar to most apartment buyers. Now, you have two options: one – you have income from work and can rent the house and pay the rent every month, or two – you can take a mortgage, and then the bank will complete the amount of money you are short of, to buy the apartment, by a loan (which bears interest, of course) that you would take, and from now on you will pay back your debt to the bank by installments, similarly to rental payments. The entire property will be used as collateral to pay the debt in case you fail to make the payments, and at the end of the period, in which you should return the loan, the house will remain your exclusive property, clear of debt – assuming that you made all of your payments in good order.

Economically, there is an interesting aspect here: it turns out that most of us (in certain countries, such as Israel, this is most of the population) invest most of our money in the residential market, and even supplement it with considerable amounts that we borrow – and now we become indebted for many years.

If the value of the property rises, we clearly have a high potential for profits – but this is only one of many investment tracks. In the long run, it is much more profitable to invest in another track (for example, in widely diversified stocks) than in the real estate market (it is certainly less dangerous than investing in a single specific property, at a single specific location), but if you tell your acquaintances about someone who took all of his savings - $150,000 – and borrowed another $150,000 from the bank in order to invest $300,000 in stocks, the common reaction (perhaps your reaction, too) will be that this person is an adventurer, a risk-lover, an irresponsible and imprudent person.

Conversely, if you hear of another person, who took all of his savings and borrowed a large amount of money from the bank to buy a house, this will seem reasonable and rational to you. You will probably not change your mind even if I play with the amounts against that person – say that he only has $90,000 and borrows $210,000 from the bank to purchase the property.

Now that you see things a bit differently, you may ask when it is correct to take a mortgage.

Well, the most basic answer (which is a pretty faulty rule of thumb, if you apply the principles I tried to impart so far), is that the cost of the monthly installments for the mortgage should under no circumstances exceed the rental fees you would have paid for a similar apartment.

What do I mean? One cannot avoid residential expenses – whether it is rental fees or a mortgage, or you are lucky enough to live in a house you own, with no mortgage. You could have rented it out, and this lost income is the cost of your own residence. Of course, the amount of the mortgage installments is a function of the amounts you saved before making the purchase, and this is also the problem with this rule of thumb: a lower installment rate necessarily means bigger savings, which could have yielded a higher potential income for the saver.

Anyway, to complete this rule of thumb, I would add another tiny rule: take the mortgage only if you have a reason to assume that the value of the apartment that you purchase is expected to rise markedly during the loan period (for example, if you intend to take a 15-year mortgage, you should not only expect the property to maintain its value for 15 years, but also estimate that it has good chances to even double or treble its value. This will give you an added value beyond the benefits of residence and the use of the property while avoiding expenses (of course, except for the interest that you will pay to the bank). By the way, this was very true for the way things were in Israel in 2006 or 1996. Nowadays, in 2016, it is far from simple to find a residential property with such characteristics, even though the prevailing interest rates are currently ideal for a mortgage).

The problem with mortgages is that the borrower takes almost all of the risk (at least with the customary model. I do not refer here to non-recourse loans, in which the borrower has no liability and the only risk is the initial amount invested in purchasing the property, as the property is the only collateral available to the lending institute. The State of Israel is the exception in this sense. In most countries, a loan or a credit line to purchase a property are non-recourse by default. The borrower is not a guarantor for the loan, and neither he nor his other assets may become a target for collection in case of default. In a non-recourse loan, the borrower introduces equity – generally quite limited – in order to purchase the property, and the property is the only collateral the bank (or the financing entity) has for the loan. In this wise, the investor only risks the equity he put in the specific asset, and even failure to repay the loan does not endanger the investor, his other assets, his other investments or his good reputation). Therefore, the potential for becoming wealthy by taking a mortgage is relatively low, unless one brilliantly picks a relatively cheap property, with potential for appreciation within a short period. Of course, this has happened before, but this scenario should definitely not be left to chance.

By the way, regarding residence – generally, the areas with the highest potential for appreciation are not among the best and most prestigious. It is generally quite the opposite. If this is not just an investment, but rather a property you wish to live in, profits come with a further "price tag" – the fact that you and your family will live in an inferior area for many years – a fact that may also influence the education of your children. Therefore, one must think much more broadly than just about finances, before taking a loan of this type.

And returning to our main subject (becoming wealthy) – the advantage in taking loans and leveraging (also for the short term, but mainly for the long term) is the potential for profits.

To illustrate this: let us say that you can pick and choose your investments and gain a phenomenal 1,000% yield, over ten years, for your investments in that period. If you initially have $15,000 to invest, your savings at the end of the period will amount to $165,000.

Pay close attention: had you borrowed an additional $15,000, you would have had $330,000 at the end of the period, and if the ratio was more extreme, of the type mostly seen in mortgages (for example, an 80%/20% ratio), you would have had to borrow $60,000 and at the end of the period you would have $825,000, no less – and all from exactly the same initial amount!

Some will still say that they risk a considerable amount of money for the promised gains, but usually the risk is not real – except in tough periods, where stocks are wiped out.

If these are non-recourse loans, this is an entirely different situation – the risk is limited to the first $15,000 (that are ventured in any case, in all possible scenarios), and the gains are fantastic.

THE TOOLBOX FOR CHAPTER EIGHTEEN – MORTGAGES AND WEALTH, AND A LITTLE MORE ON SELF-DISCIPLINE

In order to obtain considerable profits without significant equity, one must take loans.

The supposedly "conservative" approach is irrational, and those who enthusiastically voice it sometimes borrow a large amount with exposure to a specific market and a specific property, by taking a mortgage. The risk inherent in this type of loan greatly exceeds the risk in many other, alternative tracks.

Another piece of advice: in any investment track, if you can obtain a non-recourse loan, seize it with both hands.

And one last piece of advice: do not slack on self-discipline. Over time, the yield in most markets (especially the stock market, but also the real estate markets in the developed countries) is much higher than the cost of the interest on a loan. This rule especially applies to periods, in which the interest rate is close to zero and can be contractually "anchored" for a long period of time. It is important to maintain the loans for their full duration and not be scared by downward trends, financial crises or current financing needs. Nevertheless, one should never reach a "cashflow crisis" or sacrifice the long term for short-term goals or momentary pressures.

CHAPTER 19

Who Are the Friends of a Wealthy Man?

Friends. Such a common, simple and widely-used word, but with so many meanings.

You will certainly agree with me that true friends are hard to come by. How different those friends are from any other social circle we participate in, and how important they are in our lives. In our essence, as human beings, we are all social creatures deep inside (and some of us, also a lot on the outside). If this piece of information is not clear to you, this chapter will be meaningless to you and you are invited to skip it. Seriously, I'm not kidding.

This statement becomes clearer in the context of finding a mate – in many senses, our ultimate and closest friend. Spouses cross the border between social circles and family and belong to both groups at the same time. I will not discuss this type of friendship in this chapter or anywhere else in the book – so many books, films and human thinking revolves around couples and love, so it will be useless for me to go there as well. I will only mention that quite a few of us will go through their lives without knowing what true love is, and an even greater number will devote endless resources to finding love – with full or partial success, or with no success at all.

But how are friends related to success? Well, those two concepts are very intimately linked.

Let us start with the obvious: When someone has strong and/or capable friends, he has much greater chances to succeed. Personal connections can affect success in many ways, and "favoritism" is not a bad word.

An illustrative example: Let us say that you are an attorney (I wonder why I picked exactly this example…) and you have a good childhood friend, who is the CEO of a successful high-tech company with a thousand employees. His company requires legal services - it needs assistance in patent registration, for example. Even though this is a relatively small part of the activities of your friend's company, this is still significant and will become a very nice source of income for the law firm chosen for the task, not to mention the great jump in the reputation of the office that will work with such an esteemed and coveted client. Obviously, your friend will prefer to work with you, not so? You can be trusted more than a stranger! It may well be that under normal circumstances, your office would be struggling for years on the road to success, but thanks to your good friend, it becomes profitable right from the get-go, acquires more clients and a few years later, you are a success story in your own right.

Now to a more flagrant example (which is evident in many countries): Your good friend was appointed to a high government or municipal function. Will this help your enterprise? Quite possibly, if you understand me... In Israel, this used to be the case as well, and I'm happy to write that at least in recent years, the rule of law proves itself, eradicating prohibited practices from the government and the public service, as far as possible.

A little less flagrant or eminent example: Your friend is a famous television personality, who is regularly featured in the gossip columns in the newspapers and holds wild parties in his home. He invites wealthy people and other celebrities to his parties, so you have the opportunity to rub elbows with them and get connected to them easily, and immediately – including a warm recommendation from your good friend.

Our conclusion is clear and sharp: successful friends = much higher chances of success.

On the other hand, let us turn to the more problematic side of things: insincere friendships, which are the lot of rich and successful people. It is no secret that successful friends upgrade your chances to succeed. Quite a few people (generally of a hypocritical and less moral ilk) wish to turn the high-achievers into their "friends," not because they enjoy spending time with them or are charmed by their personalities, but simply for opportunistic reasons.

In extreme cases, this also refers to spouses. The tabloids are full of stories about ambitious women, who seduced rich and successful men and married them, not because they have hopelessly fallen in love, but because of their wealth. This part of the story does not necessarily have to be bad. As suggested by the title of this chapter, similar people connect to each other quite easily and neutralize problematic types that are foreign to their world.

In this wise, it became well-known that a strong friendship was forged between Bill Gates and Warren Buffett. Obviously, neither of them needs the other's money, reputation, influence or contacts. Here, there are higher chances for a true friendship. This closeness has also helped them overcome the generation gap between them.

Conversely, if an ordinary person tries to befriend Bill Gates, Bill will always have this disturbing thought (and for a good reason), that his new friend will ask him a favor one day, and that his kindness is, again, opportunistic.

Therefore, it is important to distinguish between true friendships and the rest. The best way to achieve this is to trust long-lasting friendships from old times – from childhood, high school, the military, university, and generally from periods, in which you were not quite as successful as you are today. Your childhood friend from elementary school spent many years with you before you became successful, and was your friend all along the way. Some would even say that he had a certain part in your success. It is not reasonable to assume that he is still by your side due to foreign interests – he never had these interests in the beginning.

Nevertheless, consider the ideas from chapter 2, on haters and jealous people. Sometimes even a good friend becomes a hater, and one of the harsh motives to this type of twist is envy. This is, by the way, another reason for you to encourage and promote your friends when you can. Sometimes a small, almost insignificant act on your part can critically help a friend. Let us return to the first example, of the high-tech company owner who became successful. He has many employees, the business is thriving and his best childhood friend has a small law firm. Why would he not help him and hire his services? Of course, such a wealthy person could obtain slightly better service elsewhere. He may find someone with more experience – but loyalty is priceless, and so are friendships and a spirit of mutual help. Maybe he will pay a little more for hiring his childhood friend, but this act may catapult his friend onto the fast track to success. Besides, if he does not do this – what kind of a friend is he? He can also pay a personal price if he refrains from helping in this type of case.

Ultimately, why do we need all of our work and all of the money and power that we amass? For whom? For our closest circles. For ourselves, of course, personally – but also for our family (I see my family as an even higher priority than myself) and friends.

One last thing before we summarize this chapter. It is worth remembering: good deeds always return to you with compound interest – and sometimes in very unexpected ways.

THE TOOLBOX FOR CHAPTER NINETEEN - WHO ARE THE FRIENDS OF A WEALTHY MAN?

- Choose your friends with care. Take care to distinguish between true friends and fake or opportunistic friendships.
- Try to have friends who are similar to you. As you want to become successful (otherwise, why did you buy this book?), your friends should also be successful.
- There is nothing wrong (quite the contrary!) with making strides with the help of your friends. Do not be ashamed to ask for help. Sometimes, your friends do not even know

that they can help. If you do not ask – you will not receive, and your silence might create unwanted indignation and envy.

- Always remember your friends and prefer them over strangers. In the long run, this always pays off.
- Always think about the maxim: "Keep your friends close and your enemies closer." Remember how easily a friend can become a bitter enemy. Friends who have become enemies have a great advantage over sworn enemies: they know you better. This is why, for example, divorce struggles are so bitter and problematic, and why they leave hard feelings that can never be assuaged.

CHAPTER 20

Health, Fitness and "Who is Wealthy"?

The opening sentence is about the dedication to spiritual wealth, while abstaining from material pleasures, beyond those required by the body to remain healthy.

As a child, I used to ask my grandfather: "Who is considered a rich person?"

Throughout the years, he always answered: "**Rich** is an acronym [in Hebrew – translator's note] of the words Eyes, Teeth, Arms and Legs" – in other words, health is the most important factor in our lives. All of us, rich and poor, royalty and ordinary people, are in this world for a very limited time. In the absence of health, there is no real meaning to the money one accumulates (of course with the important reservation, that in many cases money does lead to better health). It is better to be poor but healthy and fit, than rich, sick and crippled.

In my own thinking, I took that maxim from my grandfather, which accompanied me for many years, and added to it Seneca's famous saying. I united them into a sort of a middle ground that can serve as a motto. I see it as the correct and preferable "compromise" for a happy and healthy life. At a very early stage of my life I understood that it is important to take care of my health, but also to guard against obsession about one's health. In the final analysis, life is an equation with many unknown factors, and I have known quite a number of people who enjoyed perfect health and invested most of their time and energy in cultivating physical fitness and correct nutrition, only to ultimately die young in a horrible accident or in another unexpected event.

Nevertheless, I wouldn't say that it's better to neglect one's health, as in any case destiny has its own plans. The basic assumption should be that no extraordinary, unusual events will happen – such as accidents, crime and terrorism – otherwise we sentence ourselves to a life lived in an overly pessimistic world. Statistically, the chances of being hit by this type of unlikely event are much lower than the damages that we will almost certainly sustain due to physical neglect.

Our body is our most important tool on the road to success and to a full and happy life. We need to make the most out of it. Our body is a wondrous machine that allows us to perform an astonishing variety of actions (in my opinion, the most riveting part is of course the brain), but like any other machine we use, also the body requires proper maintenance. Try to think for a moment and recall the last time you felt really ill (if you don't have a memory of this type – good for you!). When you were feeling very bad, what was bothering you? What were you thinking about?

What were your wishes?

Did those things that worried you on the day before (for example the affairs at work, the planned weekend outing with the family, small household tasks that needed to be attended to) keep bothering you when you were sick? Probably not. Normally when we are sick, the pain, the nausea or the dizziness takes hold of us and we no longer feel like doing what was our top priority a day before. During sickness, the priorities change beyond recognition. Overcoming the sickness and the pain becomes the most important consideration and stands in the spotlight.

Even people who neglect their health in the most flagrant manner are not sick all the time – but those who neglect themselves – their nutrition, their hygiene and their physical fitness – **are sick more often, and even when seemingly "healthy," they feel relatively bad**. Conversely, a healthy person who keeps himself physically fit is slower to tire, is able to concentrate for longer, becomes sick less often and enjoys a better quality of life. This is also manifested in such ordinary actions as walking, climbing stairs or having sex.

Critics of this attitude often remind me that there are enough cases of sick but capable people, who can reach better achievements than a healthy and less capable person. This is of course true and generally known, but think for a moment, what could that sick and capable person do if he were healthy. For example, if he could sit and concentrate for eight hours a day instead of four. What achievements could he reach? Certainly those higher than he reached while being physically challenged. Even if we assume that he would not use these four extra hours to reach a professional, scientific or financial achievement, would he not be greatly benefitted and wouldn't his quality of life improve beyond recognition with four extra hours spent with his family, or four hours of excruciating pain that he would be spared? In many senses, quality of life derives from one's health and physical performance.

This is the last chapter of the book. I hope that you are not yet exhausted. This chapter was written to deliver a single message: **Take care of your health, but don't become obsessive about it.**

THE TOOLBOX FOR CHAPTER TWENTY - HEALTH, FITNESS AND "WHO IS WEALTHY"?

It is advisable to make your top priority keeping yourself in a good state of health and enjoying good nutrition. Other matters come later. Even at the height of overload and stress, it is always important to dedicate time and resources to the body. As they used to say in Sparta, "A healthy mind in a healthy body." This maxim contains a lot of wisdom.

You know your body better than anyone else. When a suspicious sign of a health problem appears, contact a doctor and do the necessary exams – of course, in the right proportions. One need not become obsessive about health or become a hypochondriac. Watch your nutrition, but also here, do not become fanatical. It is OK to have a hearty meal from time to time.

Be sure to exercise and keep in good shape. You don't need to be fantastically fit, especially considering our Western lifestyle, which requires almost no physical effort (of course, if you are an athlete this is completely different – but most of our readers are not). Obviously, physical functions are subject to a certain decline with age. This is natural and normal, but it is important to keep this decline gradual and under control. Some of us are lucky enough

(see Shimon Peres, of blessed memory) to keep a high level of performance until the very last moment, even after they turn 80 (or 90, or 93!).

Regarding the financial aspect of health, do not rush to save on food! Eat high-quality food as much as possible. "Saving" here will cost you dearly later on. Do not "save" on health insurance either. If, God forbid, you need medical care, it is important that you always receive swift, high-quality treatment.

Perhaps most importantly – don't be lazy! Many people have "no energy" to take care of their health or their nutrition after an overloaded, exhausting day. Work, children, travel, stress – are all very erosive to our modern Western lifestyle.

For many of us, taking care of our nutrition and investing another hour at the end of the day or during it to stay fit, seems like going one step too far - but don't go easy on yourselves. For some unclear reason, most of us are very comfortable with neglecting ourselves, of all people. We take good care of our loved ones, we pamper them, take care of their health and give them nothing but the very best – but with all of the stress factors, we forget that we also have needs and also need care.

CHAPTER 21

A Closing Prayer – Nineteen Commandments

This is the concluding chapter of the book. I actually did not plan to end the book here – I planned three additional chapters, and even prepared beautiful headings and interesting contents for them, but I finally decided to end here, because I believe in the contents of this book and act according to its guidelines, one of which is **heed the advice of wise people**. There are those who have told me that the book contains plenty of important information, is interesting and "feels" right – but that it is already overloaded with details as it is. Apart from advising me to stop writing at this point, they gave me another piece of advice: to prepare a list of simple rules – conclusions drawn from everything written so far – and present them as a "ten commandments" of sorts, summarizing the insights in this book and delivering a clear message to the readers.

Therefore, these is what this chapter contains – nineteen rules for success (I did not manage to cut it down to ten commandments… I tried to go for eighteen rules [in Jewish culture, this number is a well-known symbol for "life" – translator's note], but even this did not work out… an additional rule "worked its way" in).

But before presenting the nineteen commandments, a few words on the three additional chapters that I planned to write.

The first among them should have started with the well-known Latin maxim: "Aut Caesar aut nihil," freely translated into English as – "Either an emperor or nothing," meaning – do not accept anything other than first place. I planned to write about this – how important it is to always aim high – the highest.

As an opening statement for the second chapter, I chose the motto: "Nunquam periclum sine periclo vincitur," freely translated into English as – "Without taking a risk, you will not be saved from danger" (Publilius Syrus, "Sententiae"). Here I planned to extol taking risks (calculated risks, of course), and explain why conservatism and risk-aversion are a financial error.

The opening statement for the third and last chapter that remained outside this book was: "Hon successus alit, possunt quia posse videntur," freely translated into English as: "Those who believe in their abilities rise high and success pursues them" (Virgil, Aeneid). This short chapter was meant to address the importance of your belief in yourselves, because without it you will repeatedly fail. Here, I planned to bring examples of people, who were not blessed with outstanding abilities, but still managed to succeed thanks to their belief in themselves, ultimately exhibiting qualities that they had originally lacked. You may call this "the power of faith."

Okay – we have reached the rules, the "commandments." Some will say that it pays to buy this book only for the following lines, which summarize its entire essence – but I feel that what stands behind the rules has great value, and if you have read this far, I hope that you share this view with me. Anyway, let us continue to that part, the closing prayer of the book.

THE NINETEEN COMMANDMENTS
FOR SUCCESS

1. **Purchase adequate insurance policies.** This is the rule of thumb: dedicate 5% of your net income to this important need.

2. **Check if you have haters and people who are jealous of you.** Of course, this is not an invitation to create such people from nothing, but a lack of haters and jealous people indicates that you are not going in the right direction and are in urgent need of change.

3. **Take calculated risks. If you fail – accept it in the right proportions.** Always remember that you and your loved ones will die one day, and that there is no way to avoid this. After you equanimously accept this fact and live with it every day, there is no reason to fear risks.

4. **To succeed, nothing is more important than the first impression.** Invest in your efforts to impress. Even an artificially-created impression can become a real one.

5. **Learn to trust other people.** Only they will make you wealthy. If you do not overcome your fears in this regard,

you will greatly diminish your chances of success.

6.   **Create a personal image even when you are not there.** An image is part of the first impression. Sometimes, an image is even more important than the first impression, because the first impression is actually its by-product, in most situations in life.

7.   **Your money is worth much more when you are young; therefore, save and tighten your belt at a young age.** When you reach the age of retirement, you will be able to afford to be wasteful. Every dollar you waste during your youth may be worth tens of dollars when you grow old. Conservatism and good saving practices will lead you to success in almost every scenario, and in any case they help you diversify your risks.

8.   **Let people know about your achievements and actions.** Remember the most important maxim: "You did but failed to tell – you didn't do!" For your success, it is critical to create public relations for the things you did. Sometimes, they contribute the most to your success – even more than the work itself.

9.   **Dedicate a considerable part of your time and resources to public relations.** Yes, nothing is wrong with hiring a PR specialist, going to gala dinners and fashion shows and networking. On the contrary, the avoidance of such actions significantly reduces your chances of success.

10. **Always be patient.** Remember that haste is from the devil, or "haste makes waste." If your character collides with this advice and you are impatient by nature, force yourself into situations that require patience, for example – a long-term saving plan that involves high commissions or fines in case you break into it to immediately enjoy the benefits.

11. **Prepare a contingency plan and make daily sacrifices, to ensure that it is feasible.** Sometimes, whether you like it or not, things will not go the way you planned. Be prepared and ready (and take actual steps) to ensure that you remain at least financially comfortable even if your main plans keep going the wrong way again and again and again throughout the years.

12. **Shame is folly. Shame due to failure is even greater folly.** Let other people be ashamed, and regarding failure – it is more shameful not to try, than to try and fail. Sometimes failure is actually something to be proud of - proud to have tried and to have had the courage to pursue your dreams. You did not chicken out – your makeup is much better and stronger than that.

13. **Wastefulness and gambling are synonymous with stupidity.** If you do this, the younger you are, the more stupid you are. There is this well-known saying: "There is no fool like an old fool" – well, there is: a young fool…

14. **Invest in expanding your general knowledge. Avoid being

stuck with a single field of knowledge. I promise you that you will also enjoy life more – you will certainly enjoy your interactions with other people more, not to mention increasing your chances of success. Perhaps most importantly – it is easier to acquire plenty of general knowledge than to become more proficient in a specific field of knowledge, in which you are already quite professional. At that point you gain more by investing in general knowledge.

15. **The law and accounting are your best friends**. Never knowingly break the law. Remember that it is usually possible to reach a desired business result in a legal, legitimate manner. The system was built and is maintained by strong people, who wish to preserve their foundation of strength. Exploit the laws that they created for your own benefit, to achieve an advantage over your competitors. Use the system and harness it to your benefit.

16. **Do not save on professionals – hire the services of the best.** Always hire high-quality professionals and do not save on expenses of this type. Just as you would never choose a surgeon for your child only because he is the cheapest, do not compromise in other areas where the results are important to you.

17. **Nothing is wrong with loans and leveraging, so long as you choose loans that you can afford to repay.** Without loans and leveraging, your ability to succeed becomes much smaller. These tools can help you achieve a level of

financial strength that was not available to you before, and you will enjoy all of the profits yourself. Nevertheless, this involves considerable risk, and one should weigh every aspect of such a leveraged transaction (and use the services of the appropriate professionals).

18. **Support your friends and be their support**. In selecting professionals, always prioritize your friends. Don't hesitate to ask for their help. There is no shame in doing this. This is one of the reasons they are there, and this is also the measure of a true friendship.

19. **Take care of your health and strengthen your body**. The chances of an unhealthy person to succeed are lower, and so is his ability to enjoy the fruits of his success. If you understand that you need to maintain your car and that you should not try to save on this, what should you say about the maintenance of your body?

Epilogue

It took quite a while to write this book. Almost three years, actually. My life underwent many twists and turns during these years, but the principles according to which I conduct myself and which you have read of in this book, have not changed a bit, and I have stuck to them even more intensively. After that, the book was laid aside for several years, until I decided to publish it – and now even today, all of the principles it contains have stood the test of time.

I hope that you assimilate the principles expressed in this book and use them for your own success. This is a difficult and challenging road. It is not simple, sometimes even disappointing and not rewarding, but in the spirit of that famous saying from Bahad 1, which I believe with all of my heart – **Only he who dares and persists wins.**